FIGHT
FOR YOUR
TERRITORY

**"I have fought the good fight,
I have finished the race,
I have kept the faith."**
2 Timothy 4:7."

Joseph B. Omosigho

Dedication

This book is dedicated to God Almighty our King, whose written Word is our life manual, living standard, relationship, and territorial operations constitution. I am also dedicating to all church leaders worldwide who are laboring to see God glorified in their assigned calling, families, and territories, to expand God's kingdom here on earth, and to depopulate the kingdom of darkness. This book is also dedicated to all Christians who are victims of territorial spirits/fake pastors, false prophets, and heretic teachers' attacks and manipulations. We are in this fight together, and we will fight the good fight of faith to recover all Satan has stolen from us via evil yokes, burdens, and attacks of discouragement by God's grace, in Jesus' name.

Acknowledgements

I give all the glory to God Almighty for his unfailing grace, mercy, and favor toward me and my family. I thank my wife, Gloria; our children: David; Samuel, Hannah, and Moses, for their love and support. I also acknowledge and thank everyone who assisted and supported this work in any way. I pray this book will help you become the man or woman of courage and dominion God created. To possess your possession in the land of the living, you must fight the good fight of faith and win. I pray you will not fail God, your family, and the body of Christ in the fight against territorial spirits and enemies of our joy, peace, and prosperity, in Jesus' name. Peace!

Table of Contents

Introduction

Whether occupied or empty, a form of government often governs each territory, physically or spiritually. Humans and spiritual forces govern the physical realm, and spiritual forces govern the spiritual realm but can be influenced by humans by God's grace or via demonic relationships. We have earthly kings, presidents, governors, city mayors, and community leaders who oversee or are in control of and influence or preside over our cities, states, and nations. So too, there are hierarchies or levels of leadership in the spirit realm or the demonic world operating and influencing the affairs of our territories. There are regional and continental powers and rulers in the spirit realm too. The Book of Daniel chapter ten is an example of a territorial spirit in operation.

"Then behold, a hand touched me and set me unsteadily on my hands and knees. So, he said to me, "O Daniel, you highly regarded and greatly beloved man, understand the words that I am about to say to you and stand upright, for I have now been sent to you." And while he was saying this word to me, I stood up trembling. Then he said to me, "Do not be afraid, Daniel, for from the first day that you set your heart on understanding this and on humbling yourself before your God, your words were heard, and I have come in response to your words. But the prince of the kingdom of Persia was standing in opposition to me for twenty-one days. Then, behold, Michael, one of the chiefs [of the celestial] princes, came to help me, for I had been left there with the kings of Persia." Daniel 10:10-13.

The Kingdom of Persia Covers a Big Territory

"Now in the first year of Cyrus king of Persia—in order to fulfill the word of the Lord by the mouth of Jeremiah, the Lord stirred up the spirit of Cyrus king of Persia, so that he sent a proclamation throughout his kingdom, and also put it in writing, saying, "Thus says Cyrus king of Persia: 'The Lord, the God of heaven, has given me all the kingdoms of the earth,

and He has appointed me to build Him a house in Jerusalem, which is in Judah. Whoever there is among you of all His people, may the Lord his God be with him, and let him go up [to Jerusalem]." 2 Chronicles 36: 22-23.

Territorial Spirits Can Be Strong and Powerful

If the Prince of Persia was able to stand up against the angel of God and prevent Daniel's prayers from being answered during his fasting and prayer, just imagine what would happen if Daniel wasn't praying and fasting? Territorial spirits are incredibly strong and powerful, but they can be overcome only by the power of God. As a result, we must remain steadfast in our faith and fight for Christ's dominion over our lands, taking back all that the territorial spirits have stolen from us. This book was inspired by God to serve as a wake-up call, urging us to battle like Prophet Jeremiah and never give up on our faith. *"My soul, my soul! I writhe in anguish and pain! Oh, the walls of my heart! My heart is pounding and throbbing within me; I cannot be silent, for you have heard, O my soul, the sound of the trumpet, the alarm of war. News of one [terrible] disaster comes close after another, for the whole land is devastated; suddenly my tents are spoiled and destroyed, my [tent] curtains [ruined] in a moment. How long [O Lord] must I see the banner [marking the way for flight] and hear the sound of the trumpet [urging the people to run for safety]?"* Jeremiah 4:19-21.

Territorial or evil spirits are responsible for most negative occurrences in our homes and communities. Therefore, certain city areas are known for crime, human trafficking, poverty, prostitution, accidents, premature death, natural disasters, and limitations. How-ever, it is important to remember that Satan is not all-powerful, all-present, or all-knowing, which only God possesses attributes. Satan can carry out his plans on a global scale by dele-gating tasks, networking, and utilizing systematic and strategic leadership to work out his schemes globally.

Chapter 1

What is Territory?

A territory is a specific area of land or space. Territory can also refer to a location, or a place belonging to a person, animal, institution, or government, including but not limited to aquatic and air spaces. A territory could also be an area of land that belongs to a city, state, or nation. There are three main physical geographical categories of territories and four spiritual categories. **Physically**: We have the air, land, and sea. **Spiritually:** We have the heavens, the air, land, and sea.

Physical and Spiritual Realms Divisions
1. **Our personal and family spaces:** Our homes or family dwellings.
2. **Business or Home Office Spaces: A** place beside our dwellings, including a farm, external and home offices, or business locations.
3. **Government spaces:** Government control areas. Local, city, state, and national places or boundaries.
4. **Independent spaces:** Landmass, air, and sea spaces shared by multiple nations, like the international waters, air, and land spaces.

God created the earth as an extensive territory with everything necessary to support humankind. God later created Adam and Eve and placed them in the Garden of Eden within the earth as their business space. In the garden, Adam and Eve created their own personal and family place or area, a dwelling, and they made another spot or place as their administrative place. Although Adam and Eve had personal and business territories, they were given the whole earth to govern, but the galaxies were independent. No humans have control over the moon and stars. Only God has control over the moon and stars. They are independent but totally under God's authority.

"Then God said, "Let Us make man in Our image, according to Our likeness; let them have dominion over the fish of the sea, over the birds of the air, and over the cattle, over all the earth and over every creeping thing that creeps on the earth." So, God created man in His own image; in the image of God, He created him; male and female He created them. Then God blessed them, and God said to them, "Be fruitful and multiply; fill the earth and subdue it; have dominion over the fish of the sea, over the birds of the air, and over every living thing that moves on the earth." Genesis 1: 26-28.

Satan's War Goals Against You and Me

Jesus came to earth to battle and go to war with Satan, to redeem mankind from his slavery. The battle was won when Jesus died and was resurrected, but the war will continue until the end of time. Jesus exposed Satan's classified secret and mission in John 10: 10a. *"The thief comes only in order to steal, and kill, and destroy."*

1. To steal our joy (Take away whatever makes us happy or gives us pleasure through lies, manipulation or by force).

2. To kill our peace (kill anything or anyone that gives us rest, comfort and protection through lies, manipulation or by force).

3. To destroy our love and relationship with God. To hinder, frustrate, and trouble anyone who has a desire to show us mercy, kindness, or compassion. This he accomplishes daily by causing fear, confusion, anger, and hate.

Satan's War Goal at Work in Job's Life

All of Satan's three goals were achieved when he attacked, tempted, and afflicted Job.

1. He stole Job's joy by destroying everything Job had.
2. He killed all of Job's children in one day.

3. He destroyed Job's relationship with his wife.

"Now there was a day when Job's sons and daughters were eating and drinking wine in their oldest brother's house, and a messenger came to Job and said, "The oxen were plowing and the donkeys were feeding beside them, and the Sabeans attacked and swooped down on them and took away the animals. They also killed the servants with the edge of the sword, and I alone have escaped to tell you." While he was still speaking, another [messenger] also came and said, "The fire of God (lightning) has fallen from the heavens and has burned up the sheep and the servants and consumed them, and I alone have escaped to tell you." While he was still speaking, another [messenger] also came and said, "The Chaldeans formed three bands and made a raid on the camels and have taken them away and have killed the servants with the edge of the sword, and I alone have escaped to tell you."

While he was still speaking, another [messenger] also came and said, "Your sons and your daughters were eating and drinking wine in their oldest brother's house, and suddenly, a great wind came from across the desert, and struck the four corners of the house, and it fell on the young people and they died, and I alone have escaped to tell you." Then Job got up and tore his robe and shaved his head [in mourning for the children], and he fell to the ground and worshiped [God]. So, Satan departed from the presence of the LORD and struck Job with loathsome boils and agonizingly painful sores from the sole of his foot to the crown of his head. And Job took a piece of broken pottery with which to scrape himself, and he sat [down] among the ashes (rubbish heaps). Then his wife said to him, "Do you still cling to your integrity [and your faith and trust in God, without blaming Him]? Curse God and die!" But he said to her, "You speak as one of the [spiritually] foolish women speak [ignorant and oblivious to God's will]. Shall we indeed accept [only] good from God and not [also] accept adversity and disaster. In [spite of] all this Job did not sin with [words from] his lips." Job 1: 13-20; 2: 7-10.

Other Words Used for Territories Are

1. **Jurisdiction:** It is a place, territory, or sphere of activity over which the legal authority of a court or other institutions can exact or extends their power of influence.

"When Pilate heard it, he asked whether the man was a Galilean. And when he learned that He belonged to the jurisdiction of Herod [Antipas, the tetrarch of Galilee], he sent Him to Herod, who was also in Jerusalem at that time."
Luke 23:6-7.

2. **Region:** It is a place, area, or divided part of a state, country, or world with definable characteristics with or without fixed boundaries depending on its complexities—for example, African or Asia regions.

"Now when Jesus went into the region of Caesarea Philippi, He asked His disciples, "Who do people say that the Son of Man is?" Matthew 16:13.

3. **Habitation or Dwelling Place:** It is a house. A street, a community, a town, a province, a city, a state, a country, a region, a continent, the earth or world, and the universe. These are self-explanatory, as you and I live and dwell in them daily.

"Then the king told Zadok, "Take the ark of God back to [its rightful place in] the city [of Jerusalem, the capital]. If I find favor in the Lord's sight, He will bring me back again and let me see both it and His dwelling place (habitation)."
2   Samuel 15:25.

4. **Enclave or Portion:** It is a place or an area of a territory. It exists within a city, state, or nation, surrounded by a more extensive territory whose inhabitants are culturally or ethnically distinct in character from those surrounding areas.

"Now Joshua was old and advanced in years, and the Lord said to him, "You have grown old and advanced in years, and very substantial (Enclave), portions of the land remain to be possessed." Joshua 13:1.

5. **Colony:** It is an area inside a county or country under another county or country's total or partial political control. The United Kingdom, for example, has many colonies where the Queen or King is considered Head of State.

"So, setting sail from Troas, we ran a direct course to Samothrace, and the next day [went on] to Neapolis; and from there [we came] to Philippi, which is a leading city of the district of Macedonia, a Roman colony. We stayed on in this city for several days." Acts 16:11-12.

6. **Possession:** To own, have or to be legally in control of a thing, a place, or an asset. To oversee or own.

"I will bring you to the land which I swore to give to Abraham, Isaac, and Jacob (Israel); and I will give it to you as a pos-session. I am the Lord [you have the promise of My changeless omnipotence and faithfulness]." Exodus 6:8.

7. **Domain:** To have control, power, and authoritative influence over a given area, place, entity, government, or organization, collectively or individually.

"Prepare and dedicate the nations for war against her—The kings of Media, with their governors and commanders, and every land of their dominion." Jeremiah 51:28.

Chapter 2

How Satan Took Over Our Territory Part 1

"The seventy returned with joy, saying, "Lord, even the demons are subject to us in Your name." He said to them, "I watched Satan fall from heaven like [a flash of] lightning." Luke 10: 17-18.

How It All Began

The battle for the control of our territory—the earth, did not start today. It began when God breathed life into Adam and gave him dominion over all the works of His hands. You see, the creation of man did not go down well with Lucifer. He thought he was God's favorite until God created man. Lucifer/Satan allowed jealousy to get the best of him. Jealousy led to lust. Lust gave birth to pride, pride created comparison, and comparison led to competition against man, the likeness of God.

Lucifer's pride fed his anger, which developed into bitterness against God and man. Satan hated man with a great passion. He declared war against humankind with a mandate and a mission to steal, kill, and destroy. Satan was so mad that he became passionately desperate, consumed with bitterness. He was willing to do anything to put enmity between God and humankind. His evil intention turned him from a worshiper into an accuser.

"What is man that You are mindful of him, and the son of [earthborn] man that You care for him? Yet You have made him a little lower than God, and You have crowned him with glory and honor. You made him to have dominion over the works of Your hands; You have put all things under his feet, all sheep,

and oxen, and also the beasts of the field, the birds of the air, and the fish of the sea, whatever passes through the paths of the seas." Psalms 8: 4-8.

Satan Wanted God's Territory and Plotted a Coup

As Satan's anger and bitterness grew, he became enraged and crossed the line when he suddenly became violent and wanted to take God's throne or place but failed. Through skillful tactics, deceptive intelligence, and manipulative con games, Satan persuaded one-third of God's angels in heaven to agree to fight against God. The evil team waged battles and war against God's loyal angels but was defeated; they were banished from heaven, banished to the earth, and bound to hell.

"And war broke out in heaven, Michael [the archangel] and his angels waging war with the dragon. The dragon and his angels fought, but they were not strong enough and did not prevail, and there was no longer a place found for them in heaven. And the great dragon was thrown down, the age-old serpent who is called the devil and Satan, he who continually deceives and seduces the entire inhabited world; he was thrown down to the earth, and his angels were thrown down with him. Then I heard a loud voice in heaven, saying.

Now the salvation, and the power, and the kingdom (dominion, reign) of our God, and the authority of His Christ have come; for the accuser of our [believing] brothers and sisters has been thrown down [at last], he who accuses them and keeps bringing charges [of sinful behavior] against them before our God, day, and night. And they overcame and conquered him because of the blood of the Lamb and because of the word of their testimony, for they did not love their life and renounce their faith even when faced with death. Therefore rejoice, O heavens and you who dwell in them [in the presence of God]. Woe to the earth and the sea, because the devil has come down to you in great wrath, knowing that he has only a short time [remaining]!" Revelation 12: 7-12.

Satan Did Not Give Up, He Influenced Man Against God

It is important to note that Satan's goal and strategy have remained consistent throughout history. His focus is on influencing humankind against God through the use of his powerful tools of lies, fear, manipulation, and deception. He has been known to use half-truths to convince people to buy into his destructive network of lies, as was the case with Eve in the Garden of Eden. By appearing harmless through the guise of a beautiful serpent, he was able to manipulate Eve into disobeying God. His ultimate goal was to take over Man's territory, not because he cared about her or wanted to know what God said. It is important to remain vigilant against Satan's manipulative tactics and to always seek the truth in all situations.

"Now the serpent was more crafty (subtle, skilled in deceit) than any living creature of the field which the Lord God had made. And the serpent (Satan) said to the woman, "Can it really be that God has said, 'You shall not eat from any tree of the garden'?" And the woman said to the serpent, "We may eat fruit from the trees of the garden, except the fruit from the tree which is in the middle of the garden. God said, 'You shall not eat from it nor touch it, otherwise you will die.'" But the serpent said to the woman, "You certainly will not die! For God knows that on the day you eat from it your eyes will be opened [that is, you will have greater awareness], and you will be like God, knowing [the difference between] good and evil."

And when the woman saw that the tree was good for food, and that it was delightful to look at, and a tree to be desired in order to make one wise and insightful, she took some of its fruit and ate it; and she also gave some to her husband with her, and he ate. Then the eyes of the two of them were opened [that is, their awareness increased], and they knew that they were naked; and they fastened fig leaves together and made themselves coverings." Genesis 3: 1-7.

Satan Knows God and Believe His Word

Believers are not the only ones who know and believe God's word, Satan does too. He can even quote scriptures, but in a negative way and with the intent to deceive and promote his lies—evil games. Satan knows God hates sin and that His eyes are too holy to behold iniquity. So, he uses sin to tempt, entrap, ensnare, and enslave humankind to turn them against God to gain access into our lives to steal, kill, and destroy.

"You believe that God is one; you do well [to believe that]. The demons also believe [that], and shudder and bristle [in awe-filled terror—they have seen His wrath]!" James 2:19.

Satan Fights to Hinder Us from Embracing God's Word

"Listen then to the [meaning of the] parable of the Sower:
When anyone hears the word of the kingdom [regarding salvation] and does not understand and grasp it, the evil one comes and snatches away what was sown in his heart. This is the one on whom seed was sown beside the road. The one on whom seed was sown on rocky ground, this is the one who hears the word and at once welcomes it with joy; yet he has no [substantial] root in himself, but is only temporary, and when pressure or persecution comes because of the word, immediately he stumbles and falls away [abandoning the One who is the source of salvation].

And the one on whom seed was sown among thorns, this is the one who hears the word, but the worries and distractions of the world and the deceitfulness [the superficial pleasures and delight] of riches choke the word, and it yields no fruit. And the one on whom seed was sown on the good soil, this is the one who hears the word and understands and grasps it; he indeed bears fruit and yields, some a hundred times [as much as was sown], some sixty [times as much], and some thirty."

Matthew 13: 18-23.

Spiritual Warfare

Spiritual warfare is not child's play, it is a matter of life and death, especially for strong and mature Christians. The devil hits strong and mature Christians swiftly and hard to knock them down and out by all means possible without mercy. That is because, the longer they live, the more his evil kingdom either suffers or fails. This is the reason why strong Christians often die suddenly with little or no illness, or via demonically programmed drastic accidents and incidents depending on the window of opportunity Satan gets to launch a full-scale emergency attack. Daily, all mature Christians are constantly under satanic agents' monitoring with highly intelligent attitude surveillance, with a professionally engineered nearly 100% accurate high-definition magnifier binocular radar. A young Christian may do something wrong, and nothing bad may immediately happen to him or her, but if a mature Christian does the same thing, Satan will unleash all hell at once, because he knows, he may not get another chance to destroy such a terrifying and demon busting anointed one ever again.

FIGHT FOR YOUR TERRITORY

Chapter 3

How Satan Took Over Our Territory Part 2

"Be sober [well balanced and self-disciplined], be alert and cautious at all times. That enemy of yours, the devil, prowls around like a roaring lion [fiercely hungry], seeking someone to devour." 1 Peter 5:8.

While we are not to focus all our attention on Satan or seek to magnify him in any way, we must never underestimate his spiritual prowess. Satan can do damage or inflict harm, pain, and suffering in the lives of those who break the edge of God's covering over their lives through greed, lust, and pride. According to biblical concepts, one fact is that Satan is the real enemy of God's people. He is not a fairy tale or a joker. Christians have three major enemies to combat daily; ***"The world, Our flesh, and Satan."*** Satan is the worst of the three because he has mastered the technic of using the world and our flesh to defeat us through his specialized manipulative con games. Satan always seeks creative ways to devour any individual, family, or community outside his control.

"And you [He made alive when you] were [spiritually] dead and separated from Him because of your transgressions and sins, in which you once walked. You were following the ways of this world [influenced by this present age], in accordance with the prince of the power of the air (Satan), the spirit who is now at work in the disobedient [the unbelieving, who fight against the purposes of God].

Among these [unbelievers] we all once lived in the passions of our flesh [our behavior governed by the sinful self], indulging the desires of human nature [without the Holy Spirit] and [the impulses] of the [sin-ful] mind. We were, by nature, children [under the sentence] of [God's] wrath, just like the rest [of mankind]. " Ephesians 2: 1-3.

Territorial Powers Wanted to Kill Jesus at Birth

Satan possessed and influenced King Herod the Great and wanted to use him to kill Jesus when He was born to continue having power, authority, and dominion over the world's territories. When Herod was troubled about the birth of Jesus, the Bible specifically mentioned that all of Jerusalem (territory) was very concerned and troubled with him, expressing his territorial influence and dominance. Satan knew Herod did not want to share his territory with anyone, so he worked behind the scenes, using Herod as a vessel.

"Now after Jesus was born in Bethlehem of Judea in the days of Herod the king, behold, wise men from the east came to Jerusalem, saying, "Where is he who has been born king of the Jews? For we saw his star when it rose and have come to worship him." When Herod the king heard this, he was troubled, and all Jerusalem with him; Then Herod, when he saw that he had been tricked by the wise men, became furious, and he sent and killed all the male children in Bethlehem and in all that region who were two years old or under, according to the time that he had ascertained from the wise men. "
Matthew 2: 1-3, 16.

Herod Fulfilled Satan's Mission to Kill

It is said that Herod the Great was involved in the death of Jesus Christ in a very clever and strategic manner. Following his grandfather's footsteps, Herod Agrippa I also killed James to assert his territorial power and dominance. His fans were pleased with this move, which only emboldened him further. He then went on to arrest Peter, the head of the church at the time. Thankfully, the church rose and put an end to Herod's plans, saving Peter's life through the power of prayer. It is important to note that if the church had not acted in such a manner, Peter could have been killed for spreading the gospel as a criminal, which he was not.

"Now at that time Herod [Agrippa I] the king [of the Jews] arrested some who belonged to the church, intending to harm them. And he had James the brother of John put to death with a sword; and when he saw that it pleased the Jews, he proceeded to have Peter arrested as well. This was during the days of Unleavened Bread [the Passover week]. When he had seized Peter, he put him in prison, turning him over to four squads of soldiers of four each to guard him [in rotation throughout the night], planning after Passover to bring him out before the people [for execution]. So, Peter was kept in prison, but fervent and persistent prayer for him was being made to God by the church.

The very night before Herod was to bring him forward, Peter was sleeping between two soldiers, bound with two chains, and sentries were in front of the door guarding the prison. Suddenly, an angel of the Lord appeared [beside him] and a light shone in the cell. The angel struck Peter's side and awakened him, saying, "Get up quickly!" And the chains fell off his hands. The angel said to him, "Prepare yourself and strap on your sandals [to get ready for whatever may happen]." And he did so. Then the angel told him, "Put on your robe and follow me." And Peter went out following the angel. He did not realize that what was being done by the angel was real, but thought he was seeing a vision. When they had passed the first guard and the second, they came to the iron gate that leads into the city. Of its own accord it swung open for them; and they went out and went along one street, and at once the angel left him."
Acts 12: 1-10.

King Herod and his son were territorial beasts in human form. They were evil, and ardently wicked.

God's Word Has Dominion and Represents God

"I will bow down [in worship] toward Your holy temple And give thanks to Your name for Your lovingkindness and Your truth; For You have magnified Your word together with Your name. For the word of a king is authoritative and powerful, and who will say to him, "What are you doing?"" Psalm 138: 2; Ecclesiastes 8: 4.

To dominate is to have control, power, and authority over a given area or a place. So, God was the one who established this truth for us.

God Has Given Us Dominion

"Then God said, "Let Us (Father, Son, Holy Spirit) make man in Our image, according to Our likeness [not physical, but a spiritual personality and moral likeness]; and let them have complete authority **(Dominion)** *over the fish of the sea, the birds of the air, the cattle, and over the entire earth, and over everything that creeps and crawls on the earth." So, God created man in His own image, in the image and likeness of God He created him; male and female He created them. And God blessed them [granting them certain authority] and said to them, "Be fruitful, multiply, and fill the earth, and subjugate it [putting it under your power]; and rule over (dominate) the fish of the sea, the birds of the air, and every living thing that moves upon the earth." So God said, "Behold, I have given you every plant yielding seed that is on the surface of the entire earth, and every tree which has fruit yielding seed; it shall be food for you; and to all the animals on the earth and to every bird of the air and to everything that moves on the ground—to everything in which there is the breath of life—I have given every green plant for food"; and it was so [because He commanded it]."* Genesis 1: 26-30.

Adam Gave Satan the Territorial Power God Gave Him

When Adam and Eve chose to disobey God and obey the devil, unknown to them, they made themselves slaves to Satan.

Thus, after they obeyed and submitted themselves to him, he became their master. The world and all humans came under Satan's control, power, authority, and influence which means dominion. In Genesis 1: 26, God created man to have dominion, but due to sin—Satan robbed humanity of that dominion.

"Do you not know that when you continually offer yourselves to someone to do his will, you are the slaves of the one whom you obey, either [slaves] of sin, which leads to death, or of obedience, which leads to righteousness (right standing with God)? But thank God that though you were slaves of sin, you became obedient with all your heart to the standard of teaching in which you were instructed and to which you were committed. And having been set free from sin, you have become the slaves of righteousness [of conformity to God's will and purpose]. I am speaking in [familiar] human terms because of your natural limitations [your spiritual immaturity]. For just as you presented your bodily members as slaves to impurity and to [moral] lawlessness, leading to further lawlessness, so now offer your members [your abilities, your talents] as slaves to righteousness, leading to sanctification [that is, being set apart for God's purpose]. When you were slaves of sin, you were free in regard to righteousness [you had no desire to conform to God's will]. So, what benefit did you get at that time from the things of which you are now ashamed? [None!] For the outcome of those things is death!" Romans 6: 16-21.

Jesus Recognizes Satan's Dominion Over the Earth

Jesus recognizes Satan rule over the world, but never endorsed it. *"Peace, I leave with you, my peace I give to you; not as the world gives do I give to you. Let not your heart be troubled, neither let it be afraid. You have heard Me say to you, 'I am going away and coming back to you.' If you loved Me, you would rejoice because I said, 'I am going to the Father,' for My Father is greater than I. And now I have told you before it comes, that when it does come to pass, you may believe. I will no longer talk much with you, for the ruler of this world is coming, and he has nothing in Me."* John 14:27-30.

Satan Boasts of His Rulership to Jesus

"Then Jesus was led by the [Holy] Spirit into the wilderness to be tempted by the devil. After He had gone without food for forty days and forty nights, He became hungry. And the tempter came and said to Him, "If You are the Son of God, command that these stones become bread." But Jesus replied, "It is written and forever remains written, 'Man shall not live by bread alone, but by every word that comes out of the mouth of God.'" Then the devil took Him into the holy city [Jerusalem] and placed Him on the pinnacle (highest point) of the temple. And he said [mockingly] to Him, "If You are the Son of God, throw Yourself down; for it is written, 'He will command His angels concerning You [to serve, care for, protect and watch over You]'; And 'They will lift you up on their hands, So that You will not strike Your foot against a stone.'"

Jesus said to him, "On the other hand, it is written and forever remains written, 'You shall not test the Lord your God.'" Again, the devil took Him up on a very high mountain and showed Him all the kingdoms of the world and the glory [splendor, magni-ficence, and excellence] of them; and he said to Him, "All these things I will give You, if You fall down and worship me." Then Jesus said to him, "Go away, Satan! For it is written and forever remains written, you shall worship the Lord your God, and serve Him only." Matthew 4: 1-10.

Jesus Came to Deliver Us from the Dominion of Darkness

"For He has rescued us and has drawn us to Himself from the dominion of darkness, and has transferred us to the kingdom of His beloved Son, in whom we have redemption [because of His sacrifice, resulting in] the forgiveness of our sins [and the cancellation of sins' penalty]." Colossians 1:13-14.

Chapter 4

Territorial Conflicts

"For we are not fighting against flesh-and-blood enemies, but against evil rulers and authorities of the unseen world, against mighty powers in this dark world, and against evil spirits in the heavenly places." Ephesians 6: 12. NLT.

The same way there are territorial fights or conflicts in the physical realm, there are also territorial fights or conflicts in the spirit realm. Sovereignty or rulership over a territory may be acquired by several means. Territories can be acquired by force, manipulation, purchased, inherited, donation, and or by cession. Territories can also be acquired by other means, for example: by occupation, prescription, accretion, and annexation.

1. **Occupation:** This occurs when control is acquired over uncontrolled territory by a foreign state or government. Typically, it is supposed to be done peacefully and publicly through negotiation, but many states prefer to use force and coercion.
2. **Prescription:** This is the application of common law, meaning through which an empty or unoccupied territory may be occupied, and whoever occupies it for a long time can acquire it and claim ownership of it.
3. **Accretion:** The process of growth or increase, typically by the gradual accumulation of additional layers of land or matter: This process occurs when a territory expands or increases by natural processes, such as a river drying up, river deposits, or volcanic eruption.
4. **Cession:** The formal giving up of rights, property, or territory by a nation or state. This occurs when one nation voluntarily gives up territory to another,

typically via a treaty, sale, or because of a dispute or conflict settlement.

5. **Annexation:** Its purpose is to seize, forcefully take, acquire through manipulation, or coercion. This is when a territory is stolen or acquired by force or conquest, which often creates hash conditions, or consequences for the citizens of the territory.

Territories Can Be Allocated

"To the Reubenites and Gadites I gave the territory from Gilead as far as the Valley of Arnon, with the middle of the Valley as a boundary, and as far as the Jabbok River, the boundary of the sons of Ammon." Deuteronomy 3:16.

Territories Can Be Extended

"When the Lord your God extends your territory, as He promised you, and you say, 'I will eat meat,' because you want to eat meat, then you may eat meat, whatever you wish." Deuteronomy 12:20.

Territories Can Be Accessioned

"And there was strife and quarreling between the herdsmen of Abram's cattle and the herdsmen of Lot's cattle. Now the Canaanite and the Perizzite were living in the land at that same time [making grazing of the livestock difficult]. So, Abram said to Lot, "Please let there be no strife and disagreement between you and me, nor between your herdsmen and my herdsmen, because we are relatives. Is not the entire land before you? Please separate [yourself] from me. If you take the left, then I will go to the right; or if you choose the right, then I will go to the left." So, Lot looked and saw that the valley of the Jordan was well watered everywhere—this was before the Lord destroyed Sodom and Gomorrah; [it was all] like the garden of the Lord, like the land of Egypt, as you go to Zoar [at the south end of the Dead Sea]. Then Lot chose for himself all the valley

of the Jordan, and he traveled east. So, they separated from each other." Genesis 13:7-11.

Territories Can Be Appropriated
"Therefore, thus says the Lord God, "Most certainly in the fire of My jealousy (love for that which is Mine) I have spoken against the rest of the nations and against all Edom, who appropriated My land for themselves as a possession with wholehearted joy and with uttermost contempt, so that they might empty it out [and possess it] as prey." Ezekiel 36:5.

Territories Can Be Taken by Force
"The territory of the sons of Dan went beyond these; so, the sons of Dan went up to fight against Leshem (Laish) and captured it. Then they struck it with the edge of the sword and took possession of it and settled there [between the tribes of Naphtali and Manasseh]; they renamed Leshem, Dan, after the name of their father (ancestor) Dan." Joshua 19:47.

Territorial Spirit Fought Jesus
"Now when Jesus was born in Bethlehem of Judea in the days of Herod the king (Herod the Great), magi (wise men) from the east came to Jerusalem, asking, "Where is He who has been born King of the Jews? For we have seen His star in the east and have come to worship Him." When Herod the king heard this, he was disturbed, and all Jerusalem with him." Matthew 2: 1-3.

Territorial Spirits Has Been Fighting You from Birth
Territorial spirits and satanic agents can see our stars, they can tell who among us are powerful or weak, they know who we are, and the territory. They know the weight of our individual or collective anointing, spiritual influence, and dominance covers. Evil spirits in Acts chapter 19 alluded to the fact that they knew Jesus and Paul. The incident affected the whole territorial city of Ephesus. The seven sons of Sceva were not

unbelievers, they were pastor's kids, they grow up in church, but they were over-powered and disgraced because they were not prepared or trained in spiritual warfare.

"God was doing extraordinary and unusual miracles by the hands of Paul, so, that even handkerchiefs or face-towels or aprons that had touched his skin were brought to the sick, and their diseases left them, and the evil spirits came out [of them]. Then some of the traveling Jewish exorcists also attempted to call the name of the Lord Jesus over those who had evil spirits, saying, I implore you and solemnly command you by the Jesus whom Paul preaches. Seven sons of one [named] Sceva, a Jewish chief priest, were doing this. But the evil spirit retorted, "I know and recognize and acknowledge Jesus, and I know about Paul, but as for you, who are you?" Then the man, in whom was the evil spirit, leaped on them and subdued all of them and overpowered them, so that they ran out of that house [in terror, stripped] naked and wounded. This became known to all who lived in Ephesus, both Jews and Greeks. And fear fell upon them all, and the name of the Lord Jesus was magnified and exalted." Acts 19: 11-17.

Demons Beg Jesus to Stay in Their Occupied Territory

"They came to the other side of the sea, to the region of the Gerasenes. When Jesus got out of the boat, immediately a man from the tombs with an unclean spirit met Him, and the man lived in the tombs, and no one could bind him anymore, not even with chains. For he had often been bound with shackles [for the feet] and with chains, and he tore apart the chains and broke the shackles into pieces, and no one was strong enough to subdue and tame him.

Night and day, he was constantly screaming and shrieking among the tombs and on the mountains, and cutting himself with [sharp] stones. Seeing Jesus from a distance, he ran up and bowed down before Him [in homage]; and screaming with a loud voice, he said, "What business do we have in common with each other, Jesus, Son of the Most High God? I implore you by God [swear to me], do not torment me!"

For Jesus had been saying to him, "Come out of the man, you unclean spirit!" He was asking him, "What is your name?" And he replied, "My name is Legion; for we are many." And he began begging Him repeatedly not to send them out of the region. Now there was a large herd of pigs grazing there on the mountain. And the demons begged Him, saying, "Send us to the pigs so that we may go into them!" Jesus gave them permission. And the unclean spirits came out [of the man] and entered the pigs. The herd, numbering about two thousand, rushed down the steep bank into the sea; and they were drowned [one after the other] in the sea.

"The herdsmen [tending the pigs] ran away and reported it in the city and in the country. And the people came to see what had happened. They came to Jesus and saw the man who had been demon-possessed sitting down, clothed and in his right mind, the man who had [previously] had the "legion" [of demons]; and they were frightened. Those who had seen it described [in detail] to the people what had happened to the demon-possessed man, and [told them all] about the pigs.

So, the people began to beg with Jesus to leave their region. As He was stepping into the boat, the [Gentile] man who had been demon-possessed was begging with Him [asking] that he might go with Him [as a disciple]. Jesus did not let him [come], but [instead] He said to him, "Go home to your family and tell them all the great things that the Lord has done for you, and how He has had mercy on you." So, he [obeyed and] went away and began to publicly proclaim in Decapolis [the region of the ten Hellenistic cities] all the great things that Jesus had done for him; and all the people were astonished."
Mark 5:1-20.

Ten Lessons to Learn from the above Scriptures

1. The territorial powers—spirits begged Jesus not to send them away from the territory—region they were operating in.
2. The people of the land did not want Jesus in their territory, they did not want Him to operate in their domain.
3. The center point of demonic invasion—the man the demons were using to terrorize the city got his deliverance and there was peace.
4. The delivered man wanted to leave the region and follow Jesus, and Jesus refused to permit his request.
5. The demons acknowledged Jesus' authority, because they knew to ask Him if the time has come for Jesus to torment them.
6. Jesus did not send the demons out of the territory because the people were still aligned with them, thus they begged Jesus to leave their territory.
7. Jesus showed His disciples that He has authority and power over territorial spirits, and that one day, they too would be able to exercise the same power.
8. The story shows us that legions of demons can take up residence in a person. The demonic man was turned into a strong-man or strong-woman. The story shows us how a strongman can hold a whole city and region in bondage and captivity.
9. The story confirms the fact that demonic powers or evil spirits can oversee a region indirectly by inhabiting humans. If five thousand demons had taken up residence in one man, just imagine how many demons there are in a city.
10. The story shows and confirms the power of salvation, and that deliverance is possible no matter how deep anyone has gone in the doom or pit of darkness. Jesus changed the story of the demon possessed man, turned

his ashes into something beautiful, and he became a testimony of God's mercy.

Territorial Alliance Can Be Formed

"But when the people of Gibeon [the Hivites] heard what Joshua had done to Jericho and Ai, they too acted craftily and cunningly, and set out and took along provisions, but took worn out sacks on their donkeys, and wineskins (leather bottles) that were worn out and split open and patched together, and worn-out and patched sandals on their feet, and worn-out clothes; and all their supply of food was dry and had turned to crumbs.

They went to Joshua in the camp at Gilgal and said to him and the men of Israel, "We have come from a far country; so now, make a covenant (treaty) with us." But the men of Israel said to the Hivites, "Perhaps you are living within our land; how then can we make a covenant (treaty) with you?" They said to Joshua, "We are your servants." Then Joshua said to them, "Who are you, and where do you come from?" They said to him, "Your servants have come from a country that is very far away because of the fame of the Lord your God; for we have heard the news about Him and all [the remarkable things] that He did in Egypt, and everything that He did to the two kings of the Amorites who were beyond the Jordan, to Sihon the king of Heshbon and to Og the king of Bashan who lived in Ashtaroth.

So, our elders and all the residents of our country said to us, 'Take provisions for the journey and go to meet the sons of Israel and say to them, "We are your servants; now make a covenant (treaty) with us."' This bread of ours was hot (fresh) when we took it along as our provision from our houses on the day we left to come to you; now look, it is dry and has turned to crumbs. These wineskins which we filled were new, and look, they are split; our clothes and our sandals are worn out because of the very long journey [that we had to make]." So, the men [of Israel] took some of their own provisions [and offered them in friendship], and [foolishly] did not ask for the counsel of the Lord. Joshua made peace with them and made a covenant (treaty) with them, to let them live; and the leaders of the congregation [of Israel] swore an oath to them.

It happened that three days after they had made a covenant (treaty) with them, the Israelites heard that they were [actually] their neighbors and that they were living among them."
Joshua 9: 3-16.

Chapter 5

Why Territory Matter?

"When the unclean spirit comes out of a person, it roams through waterless places in search [of a place] of rest; and not finding any, it says, 'I will go back to my house (person) from which I came.' And when it comes, it finds the place swept and put in order. Then it goes and brings seven other spirits more evil than itself, and they go in [the person] and live there; and the last state of that person becomes worse than the first."
Luke 11: 24-26.

Do not be deceived by those who claim location or territory dynamics do not matter. I beg to disagree based on scriptural proof that even God knows location is essential and matters.

God promises Abram a Territory

"Now [in Haran] the Lord had said to Abram, "Go away from your country, and from your relatives and from your father's house, to the land which I will show you."
Genesis 12: 1.

Jesus was Not Born in Africa Because Territory Matter

"Now when Jesus was born in Bethlehem of Judea in the days of Herod the king (Herod the Great), magi (wise men) from the east came to Jerusalem, asking, "Where is He who has been born King of the Jews? For we have seen His star in the east and have come to worship Him." When Herod the king heard this, he was disturbed, and all Jerusalem with him. So, he called together all the chief priests and scribes of the people and [anxiously] asked them where the Christ (the Messiah, the Anointed) was to be born. They replied to him, "In Bethlehem of Judea, for this is what has been written by the prophet

[Micah]: 'And you, Bethlehem, in the land of Judah, are not in any way least among the leaders of Judah; For from you shall come a Ruler Who will shepherd My people Israel.'"
Matthew 2: 1-6.

God Has Lands for You to Possess

God had specific lands He told Joshua to possess. You and I are called to a specific area, city, or nation to do ministry as our domain, and from there, we can reach other lands for the Lord, just as Joshua did. It was God's commission to Joshua regarding the territory.

"Now it happened after the death of Moses the servant of the Lord, that the Lord spoke to Joshua the son of Nun, Moses' servant (attendant), saying, "Moses My servant is dead; now therefore arise [to take his place], cross over this Jordan, you and all this people, into the land which I am giving to them, to the sons of Israel. I have given you every place on which the sole of your foot treads, just as I promised to Moses. From the wilderness [of Arabia in the south] and this Lebanon [in the north], even as far as the great river, the river Euphrates [in the east], all the land of the Hittites (Canaan), and as far as the Great [Mediterranean] Sea toward the west shall be your territory.

No man will [be able to] stand before you [to oppose you] as long as you live. Just as I was [present] with Moses, so will I be with you; I will not fail you or abandon you. Be strong and confident and courageous, for you will give this people as an inheritance the land which I swore to their fathers (ancestors) to give them. Only be strong and very courageous; be careful to do [everything] in accordance with the entire law which Moses My servant commanded you; do not turn from it to the right or to the left, so that you may prosper and be successful wherever you go.

This Book of the Law shall not depart from your mouth, but you shall read [and meditate on] it day and night, so that you may be careful to do [everything] in accordance with all that is written in it; for then you will make your way prosperous, and then you will be successful. Have I not commanded you? Be strong and courageous! Do not be terrified or dismayed (intimidated), for the Lord your God is with you wherever you go."
Then Joshua commanded the officers of the people, saying, "Go throughout the camp and command the people, saying, 'Prepare your provisions, for within three days you are to cross this [river] Jordan, to go in to take possession of the land which the Lord your God is giving you to possess [as an inheritance].'"

To the Reubenites and to the Gadites and to the half-tribe of Manasseh, Joshua said, "Remember the word which Moses the servant of the Lord commanded you, saying, 'The Lord Your God is giving you rest (peace) and will give you this land [east of the Jordan].' Your wives, your children, and your cattle shall [be allowed to] stay in the land which Moses gave you on this [eastern] side of the Jordan, but you shall go across [the river] before your brothers (the other tribes) armed for battle, all your brave warriors, and you shall help them [conquer and take possession of their land]." Joshua 1: 1-14.

Caleb Fought to Possess His Territory

"Now these are the territories which the tribes of Israel inherited in the land of Canaan, which Eleazar the priest, and Joshua the son of Nun, and the heads of the households of the tribes of Israel apportioned to them as an inheritance, by the lot of their inheritance, as the Lord had commanded through Moses, for the nine tribes and the half-tribe. For Moses had given an inheritance to the two tribes and the half-tribe beyond the Jordan; but he did not give [any territory as] an inheritance to the Levites among them.

For the sons of Joseph were two tribes, Manasseh and Ephraim, and no portion was given in the land to the Levites except cities in which to live, with their pasture lands for their livestock and for their property. The Israelites did just as the Lord had commanded Moses, and they divided the land. Then the [tribe of the] sons of Judah approached Joshua in Gilgal, and Caleb the son of Jephunneh the Kenizzite said to him, "You know the word which the Lord said to Moses the man of God concerning me and you in Kadesh-barnea. I was forty years old when Moses the servant of the Lord sent me from Kadesh-barnea to scout the land [of Canaan], and I brought a report back to him as it was in my heart. My brothers (fellow spies) who went up with me made the heart of the people melt with fear; but I followed the Lord my God completely.

So, Moses swore [an oath to me] on that day, saying, 'Be assured that the land on which your foot has walked will be an inheritance to you and to your children always, because you have followed the Lord my God completely.' And now, look, the Lord has let me live, just as He said, these forty-five years since the Lord spoke this word to Moses, when Israel wandered in the wilderness; and now, look at me, I am eighty-five years old today. I am still as strong today as I was the day Moses sent me; as my strength was then, so is my strength now, for war and for going out and coming in. So now, give me this hill country about which the Lord spoke that day, for you heard on that day that the [giant-like] Anakim were there, with great fortified cities; perhaps the Lord will be with me, and I shall drive them out just as the Lord said." So, Joshua blessed him and gave Hebron to Caleb the son of Jephunneh as an inheritance."
Joshua 14: 1-13.

No Fight, No Possession of Territories

God promised to give us the land, but we must fight to get it. The same is true for you and me. You and I must fight to possess our possession. We must fight to dominate, occupy, and govern the lands God has allocated to us. If God gives us the land on a platter of gold, we may not value it, but when we fight to get it, we will treasure, value, and cherish the land. If we choose not to fight, we may have difficulty accomplishing anything meaningful or significant for the Lord. As Christians, we don't often fight with guns, bows, and arrows, we fight on our knees because our fight is not carnal, sensual, or physical.

"The weapons of our warfare are not physical [weapons of flesh and blood]. Our weapons are divinely powerful for the destruction of fortresses. We are destroying sophisticated arguments and every exalted and proud thing that sets itself up against the [true] knowledge of God, and we are taking every thought and purpose captive to the obedience of Christ, being ready to punish every act of disobedience, when your own obedience [as a church] is complete. For our struggle is not against flesh and blood [contending only with physical opponents], but against the rulers, against the powers, against the world forces of this [present] darkness, against the spiritual forces of wickedness in the heavenly (supernatural) places."
2 Corinthians 10:4-6; Ephesians 6:12.

When the Holy Spirit Fell, He First Fell in a Specific Place
"And, being assembled together with them, commanded them that they should not depart from Jerusalem, but wait for the promise of the Father, which, saith he, ye have heard of me. For John truly baptized with water; but ye shall be baptized with the Holy Ghost not many days hence.

When they therefore were come together, they asked of him, saying, Lord, wilt thou at this time restore again the kingdom to Israel? And he said unto them, it is not for you to know the times or the seasons, which the Father hath put in his own power. But ye shall receive power, after that the Holy Ghost is come upon you: and ye shall be witnesses unto me both in Jerusalem, and in all Judaea, and in Samaria, and unto the uttermost part of the earth.

When the day of Pentecost had come, they were all together in one place, and suddenly a sound came from heaven like a rushing violent wind, and it filled the whole house where they were sitting. There appeared to them tongues resembling fire, which were being distributed [among them], and they rested on each one of them [as each person received the Holy Spirit]. And they were all filled [that is, diffused throughout their being] with the Holy Spirit and began to speak in other tongues (different languages), as the Spirit was giving them the ability to speak out [clearly and appropriately]. Now there were Jews living in Jerusalem, devout and God-fearing men from every nation under heaven." Acts 1: 4-8; 2: 1-5.

Territory Matters, that Why There is Heaven and Hell

"Now there was a certain rich man who was habitually dressed in expensive purple and fine linen, and celebrated and lived joyously in splendor every day. And a poor man named Lazarus, was laid at his gate, covered with sores. He [eagerly] longed to eat the crumbs which fell from the rich man's table. Besides, even the dogs were coming and licking his sores. Now it happened that the poor man died, and his spirit was carried away by the angels to Abraham's bosom (paradise); and the rich man also died and was buried.

In Hades (the realm of the dead), being in torment, he looked up and saw Abraham far away and Lazarus in his bosom (paradise). And he cried out, 'Father Abraham, have mercy on me, and send Lazarus so that he may dip the tip of his finger in water and cool my tongue, because I am in severe agony in this flame.' But Abraham said, 'Son, remember that in your lifetime you received your good things [all the comforts and de-lights], and Lazarus likewise bad things [all the discomforts and distresses]; but now he is comforted here [in paradise], while you are in severe agony. And besides all this, between us and you [people] a great chasm has been fixed, so that those who want to come over from here to you will not be able, and none may cross over from there to us.'

So, the rich man said, 'Then, father [Abraham], I beg you to send Lazarus to my father's house—for I have five brothers— in order that he may solemnly warn them and witness to them, so that they too will not come to this place of torment.' But Abraham said, 'They have [the Scriptures given by] Moses and the [writings of the] Prophets; let them listen to them.' He replied, 'No, father Abraham, but if someone from the dead goes to them, they will repent [they will change their old way of thinking and seek God and His righteousness].' And he said to him, 'If they do not listen to [the messages of] Moses and the Prophets, they will not be persuaded even if someone rises from the dead.'" Luke 16: 19-31.

God Recognizes Territories

"When you come opposite the territory of the sons of Ammon, do not harass them nor provoke them, for I will not give you any of the land of the sons of Ammon as a possession, because I have given it to the sons of Lot as a possession. When the Most High gave the nations their inheritance, when He separated the sons of man, He set the boundaries of the peoples according to the number of the sons of Israel."
Deuteronomy 2:19; 32: 8.

Chapter 6

Satan's Territorial Spirits Network

"In this the children of God and the children of the devil are manifest: Whoever does not practice righteousness is not of God, nor is he who does not love his brother." 1 John 3:10.

No Fight, No Possession of Territories

"Knowing their thoughts Jesus said to them, "Any kingdom that is divided against itself is being laid waste; and no city or house divided against itself will [continue to] stand. If Satan casts out Satan [that is, his demons], he has become divided against himself and disunited; how then will his kingdom stand?" Matthew 12:25-2.

Satan's Network

"And war broke out in heaven, Michael [the archangel] and his angels waging war with the dragon. The dragon and his angels fought, but they were not strong enough and did not prevail, and there was no longer a place found for them in heaven. And the great dragon was thrown down, the age-old serpent who is called the devil and Satan, he who continually deceives and seduces the entire inhabited world; he was thrown down to the earth, and his angels were thrown down with him." Revelation 12: 7-9.

Satanic Network of Territorial Spirits

"For our struggle is not against flesh and blood [contending only with physical opponents], but against the rulers, against the powers, against the world forces of this [present] darkness, against the spiritual forces of wickedness in the heavenly (supernatural) places." Ephesians 6: 12.

Satan's Territorial Spirit Dominance

"For He has rescued us and has drawn us to Himself from the dominion of darkness, and has transferred us to the kingdom of His beloved Son." Colossians 1: 13.

Some of them Have Thrones in Cities, States, and Nations

"For by Him all things were created in heaven and on earth, [things] visible and invisible, whether thrones or dominions or rulers or authorities; all things were created and exist through Him [that is, by His activity] and for Him. And He Himself existed and is before all things, and in Him all things hold to-gether. [His is the controlling, cohesive force of the universe.]" Colossians 1: 16-17.

They Run Evil Operations Against Us

"When He had disarmed the rulers and authorities [those supernatural forces of evil operating against us], He made a public example of them [exhibiting them as captives in His triumphal procession], having triumphed over them through the cross." Colossians 2: 15.

They are a Powerful Network of Liars Promoting Lies

"You are of your father the devil, and it is your will to practice the desires [which are characteristic] of your father. He was a murderer from the beginning, and does not stand in the truth because there is no truth in him. When he lies, he speaks what is natural to him, for he is a liar and the father of lies and half-truths." John 8:44.

They are a Network of Destroyers, and Afflicters

"Then the fifth angel sounded [his trumpet], and I saw a star (angelic being) that had fallen from heaven to the earth; and the key of the bottomless pit (abyss) was given to him (the star-angel). He opened the bottomless pit, and smoke like the smoke of a great furnace flowed out of the pit; and the sun and the atmosphere were darkened by the smoke from the pit. Then

out of the smoke came locusts upon the earth, and power [to hurt] was given to them, like the power which the earth's scorpions have. They were told not to hurt the grass of the earth, nor any green thing, nor any tree, but [to hurt] only the people who do not have the seal (mark of ownership, protection) of God on their foreheads. They were not permitted to kill anyone, but to torment and cause them extreme pain for five months; and their torment was like the torment from a scorpion when it stings a man.

And in those days people will seek death and will not find it; and they will long to die [to escape the pain], but [will discover that] death evades them. The locusts resembled horses pre-pared and equipped for battle; and on their heads appeared to be [something like] golden crowns, and their faces resembled human faces. They had hair like the hair of women, and their teeth were like the teeth of lions. They had breast-plates (scales) like breastplates made of iron; and the [whirring] noise of their wings was like the [thunderous] noise of countless horse-drawn chariots charging [at full speed] into battle. They have tails like scorpions, and stingers; and in their tails is their power to hurt people for five months. They have as king over them, the angel of the abyss (the bottomless pit); in Hebrew his name is Abaddon (destruction), and in Greek he is called Apollyon (destroyer-king)." Revelation 9: 1-11.

A Network of Persecutors

"And when the dragon saw that he was thrown down to the earth, he persecuted the woman who had given birth to the male Child. But the two wings of the great eagle were given to the woman, so that she could fly into the wilderness to her place, where she was nourished for a time and times and half a time (three and one-half years), away from the presence of the serpent (Satan). And the serpent hurled water like a river out of his mouth after the woman, so that he might cause her to be swept away with the flood. But the earth helped the woman, and

the earth opened its mouth and swallowed up the river which the dragon had hurled out of his mouth. So, the dragon was enraged with the woman, and he went off to wage war on the rest of her children (seed), those who keep and obey the commandments of God and have the testimony of Jesus [holding firmly to it and bearing witness to Him]." Revelation 12: 13-17.

Their Network is United and Strong, they Collaborate well

"Now when the unclean spirit has gone out of a man, it roams through waterless (dry, arid) places in search of rest, but it does not find it. Then it says, 'I will return to my house from which I came.' And when it arrives, it finds the place unoccupied, swept, and put in order. Then it goes and brings with it seven other spirits more wicked than itself, and they go in and make their home there. And the last condition of that man becomes worse than the first. So, will it also be with this wicked generation." Matthew 12: 43-45.

They Partner with Human Networks

"When you enter the land which the Lord your God is giving you, you shall not learn to imitate the detestable (repulsive) practices of those nations. There shall not be found among you anyone who makes his son or daughter pass through the fire [as a sacrifice], one who uses divination and fortune-telling, one who practices witchcraft, or one who interprets omens, or a sorcerer, or one who casts a charm or spell, or a medium, or a spiritist, or a necromancer [who seeks the dead]. For everyone who does these things is utterly repulsive to the Lord; and because of these detestable practices the Lord your God is driving them out before you." Deuteronomy 18: 9-12.

They Have Their Own Pastors, Prophets, and Preachers

"Concerning the prophets: My heart [says Jeremiah] is broken within me, all my bones shake; I have become like a drunken man, A man whom wine has overcome, Because of the

Lord and because of His holy words [declared against unfaithful leaders]. For the land is full of adulterers (unfaithful to God); The land mourns because of the curse [of God upon it]. The pastures of the wilderness have dried up. The course of action [of the false prophets] is evil and they rush into wickedness; And their power is not right. "For both [false] prophet and priest are ungodly (profane, polluted); Even in My house I have found their wickedness," says the Lord. "Also, I have seen a horrible thing in the prophets of Jerusalem: They commit adultery and walk in lies; They encourage and strengthen the hands of evildoers. So that no one has turned back from his wickedness. All of them have become like Sodom to Me, And her inhabitants like Gomorrah. "I did not send [these counterfeit] prophets, yet they ran; I did not speak to them, yet they prophesied." Jeremiah 23: 9-11, 14, 21.

Supported by City, State and Notional Leaders

"Now Ahab told Jezebel all that Elijah had done, and how he had killed all the prophets [of Baal] with the sword. Then Jezebel sent a messenger to Elijah, saying, "So may the gods do to me, and even more, if by this time tomorrow I do not make your life like the life of one of them." And Elijah was afraid and arose and ran for his life, and he came to Beersheba which belongs to Judah, and he left his servant there."
1 Kings 19: 1-3.

Their Network Agenda Leading to Perilous Times

"Many false prophets will appear and mislead many. Because lawlessness is increased, the love of most people will grow cold. But the one who endures and bears up [under suffering] to the end will be saved. This good news of the kingdom [the gospel] will be preached throughout the whole world as a testimony to all the nations, and then the end [of the age] will come. "So, when you see the abomination of desolation [the appalling sacrilege that astonishes and makes desolate], spoken of by the prophet Daniel, standing in the Holy Place (let

the reader understand), then let those who are in Judea flee to the mountains [for refuge]. Whoever is on the housetop must not go down to get the things that are in his house [because there will not be enough time].

Whoever is in the field must not turn back to get his coat. And woe to those who are pregnant and to those who are nursing babies in those days! Pray that your flight [from persecution and suffering] will not be in winter, or on a Sabbath [when Jewish laws prohibit travel]. For at that time there will be a great tribulation (pressure, distress, oppression), such as has not occurred since the beginning of the world until now, nor ever will [again]. And if those days [of tribulation] Had not been cut short, no human life would be saved; but for the sake of the elect (God's chosen ones) those days will be shortened. Then if anyone says to you [during the great tribulation], 'Look! Here is the Christ,' or 'There He is,' do not believe it. For false Christs and false prophets will appear and they will provide great signs and wonders, so as to deceive, if possible, even the elect (God's chosen ones)."
Matthew 24:11-24.

Chapter 7

Activities of Territorial Spirits

"Then he showed me Joshua the high priest standing before the Angel of the Lord, and Satan standing at his right hand to oppose him." Zechariah 3:1.

Territorial Spirits Oppose the Gospel and Christians

Territorial spirits work relentlessly to obstruct the spread of the gospel of Christ. Some Christians team up with territorial spirits to work against other Christians to restrain or quench the light of God in them. These unbroken, unrefined, worldly Christians constantly see ways to lord it over Christians. Thus, they begin to exalt control over their homes and territories. Those who cannot break free from their grips fall prey, and their light and destiny will be suppressed or rendered ineffective. These territorial spirits aim to keep their assigned territories in perpetual darkness. They oppress and influence those living in that area to become a problem to the body of believers in that territory.

Satan made many attempts to prevent Jesus from dying for us, using worldly tactics such as greed, lust, diplomacy, craftiness, and deceptive wisdom. Jesus Himself referred to the activities of monitoring spirits in conjunction with territorial spirits in the parable of the Sower of Seed. It is sad that when some individuals attend powerful revival meetings in certain cities and become inspired by God, but only to return to their lands or domain and find that the seeds of the word that had ignited the fire of God's hunger, taste, and zeal have eaten up by the birds of the air. The fire they receive quenches before they get home to light their cities for Christ.

"He told them many things in parables, saying, "Listen care-fully: a Sower went out to sow [seed in his field]; and as he sowed, some seed fell beside the road [between the fields], and the birds came and ate it. Other seeds fell on rocky ground, where they did not have much soil; and at once they sprang up because they had no depth of soil. But when the sun rose, they were scorched; and because they had no root, they withered away. Other seeds fell among thorns, and thorns came up and choked them out. Listen then to the [meaning of the] parable of the sower: When anyone hears the word of the kingdom [regarding salvation] and does not understand and grasp it, the evil one comes and snatches away what was sown in his heart.

This is the one on whom seed was sown beside the road. The one on whom seed was sown on rocky ground, this is the one who hears the word and at once welcomes it with joy; yet he has no [substantial]root in himself, but is only temporary, and when pressure or persecution comes because of the word, immediately he stumbles and falls away [abandoning the One who is the source of salvation]. And the one on whom seed was sown among thorns, this is the one who hears the word, but the worries and distractions of the world and the deceitfulness [the superficial pleasures and delight] of riches choke the word, and it yields no fruit. " Matthew 13: 3-6, 18-22.

They Promote Sin and Crime

Territorial spirits enjoy working secretly behind the scenes but in teams. Their team of evil networks works passionately; creatively, they intentionally manipulate and turn people's hearts against God. They manipulate people into believing and embracing science fiction, logical reasoning, and physiological propaganda. Their main underlying factor is to push people to love and embrace sinful nature, lust, greed, and pride.

"Do not love the world [of sin that opposes God and His precepts], nor the things that are in the world. If anyone loves the world, the love of the Father is not in him. For all that is in

the world—the lust and sensual craving of the flesh and the lust and longing of the eyes and the boastful pride of life [pretentious confidence in one's resources or in the stability of earthly things]—these do not come from the Father, but are from the world. The world is passing away, and with it its lusts [the shameful pursuits and ungodly longings]; but the one who does the will of God and carries out His purposes lives forever." 1 John 2: 15-17.

All Wrongdoing Is Sin, Satan Thrives Where There Is Sin

The Bible states that all wrongdoing is sin according to 1 John 5:17. *"All wrongdoing is sin, and there is sin that does not lead to death [one can repent of it and be forgiven]."* Satan thrives and turns into a stronghold anywhere there is sin. Sin gives Satan and his evil forces—*Territorial spirits,* legal ground to operate freely and do more harm. Sin gives territorial spirits authority and power in our communities and cities to work through idolatry or paganism, whether animal or human rituals, war or conflicts, witchcraft, or demonic expressions. Then there are abortion or sexual perversion, human trafficking, and body parts trading. Substance abuse or alcoholism, occultism or spiritism, and adult/child pornography or sexual promiscuity. Then, there is incest or homosexuality, spouse exchange for sexual pleasure, and many other evils in these last days.

"But understand this, that in the last days dangerous times [of great stress and trouble] will come [difficult days that will be hard to bear]. For people will be lovers of self [narcissistic, self-focused], lovers of money [impelled by greed], boastful, arrogant, revilers, disobedient to parents, ungrateful, unholy and profane, [and they will be] unloving [devoid of natural human affection, calloused and inhumane], irreconcilable, malicious gossips, devoid of self-control [intemperate, immoral], brutal, haters of good, traitors, reckless, conceited, lovers of [sensual] pleasure rather than lovers of God, holding to a

form of [outward] godliness (religion), although they have denied its power [for their conduct nullifies their claim of faith].

Avoid such people and keep far away from them. For among them are those who worm their way into homes and captivate morally weak and spiritually dwarfed women weighed down by [the burden of their] sins, easily swayed by various impulses, always learning and listening to anybody who will teach them, but never able to come to the knowledge of the truth. Just as Jannes and Jambres [the court magicians of Egypt] opposed Moses, so these men also oppose the truth, men of depraved mind, unqualified and worthless [as teachers] in regard to the faith. " 2 Timothy 3: 1-8.

Territorial Spirit Causes Problems
A. They Blind the Minds of Unchristian

Territorial spirits often seek ways to use distract, cloud, or blind the eyes of our understanding as Christians. They distract, cloud, or blind the minds of unbelievers. Nowadays, people are manipulated to believe the lie that Jesus is not the only way to God, but just one of the prophets or one of the ways to heaven. *"Among them the god of this world [Satan] has blinded the minds of the unbelieving to prevent them from seeing the illuminating light of the gospel of the glory of Christ, who is the image of God."* 2 Corinthians 4:4

B. They Hinder the Salvation of People

"When they had traveled through the entire island [of Cyprus] as far as Paphos, they found a sorcerer, a Jewish false prophet named Bar-Jesus, who was [closely associated] with the [pro-consul [of the province], Sergius Paulus, an intelligent and sen-sible man. He called for Barnabas and Saul and wanted to hear the word of God [concerning eternal salvation through faith in Christ]. But Elymas the sorcerer (for that is how his name is translated) opposed them, trying to turn the proconsul away from accepting the faith." Acts 13: 6-8.

C. Create Confusion in Families and Communities

Infighting, constant quarreling, confusion, division, and disunity in our families, communities and cities are signs of territorial powers at work. Our God is not a God of confusion and disorderliness. *"For God [who is the source of their prophesying] is not a God of confusion and disorder but of peace and order. As [is the practice] in all the churches of the saints (God's people)."* 1 Corinthians 14:33.

D. They Cause and Induce Jealousy

"And if a spirit (sense, attitude) of jealousy comes over him and he is jealous and angry at his wife who has defiled herself—or if a spirit of jealousy comes over him and he is jealous of his wife when she has not defiled herself—or when a spirit (sense, attitude) of jealousy and suspicion comes on a man and he is jealous of his wife; then he shall have the woman stand before the Lord, and the priest shall apply this law to her." Numbers 5: 14, 30.

E. They Enslave People with Fear

"For you have not received a spirit of slavery leading again to fear [of God's judgment], but you have received the Spirit of adoption as sons [the Spirit producing sonship] by which we [joyfully] cry, "Abba! Father! and [that He] might free all those who through [the haunting] fear of death were held in slavery throughout their lives." Romans 8: 15; Hebrews 2: 15.

F. Manipulate Believers into Half Truths Errors

"We [who teach God's word] are from God [energized by the Holy Spirit], and whoever knows God [through personal experience] listens to us [and has a deeper understanding of Him]. Whoever is not of God does not listen to us. By this we know [without any doubt] the spirit of truth [motivated by God] and the spirit of error [motivated by Satan]. You are of your

father the devil, and it is your will to practice the desires [which are characteristic] of your father. He was a murderer from the beginning, and does not stand in the truth because there is no truth in him. When he lies, he speaks what is natural to him, for he is a liar and the father of lies and half-truths." 1 John 4:6; John 8:44.

G. They are the engine Behind False Prophets

"Beloved, do not believe every spirit [speaking through a self-proclaimed prophet]; instead test the spirits to see whether they are from God, because many false prophets and teachers have gone out into the world. By this you know and recognize the Spirit of God: every spirit that acknowledges and confesses [the fact] that Jesus Christ has [actually] come in the flesh [as a man] is from God [God is its source]; and every spirit that does not confess Jesus [acknowledging that He has come in the flesh, but would deny any of the Son's true nature] is not of God; this is the spirit of the antichrist. They [who teach twisted doctrine] are of the world and belong to it; therefore, they speak from the [viewpoint of the] world [with its immoral freedom and baseless theories—demanding compliance with their opinions and ridiculing the values of the upright], and the [gullible one of the] world listens closely and pays attention to them." 1 John 4: 1-4, 5.

H. They Do False Miracle, Fake Signs, and Wonders

"Let no one in any way deceive or entrap you, for that day will not come unless the apostasy comes first [that is, the great rebellion, the abandonment of the faith by professed Christians], and the man of lawlessness is revealed, the son of destruction [the Antichrist, the one who is destined to be destroyed], who opposes and exalts himself [so proudly and so insolently] above every so-called god or object of worship, so that he [actually enters and] takes his seat in the temple of God, publicly proclaiming that he himself is God. Do you not

remember that when I was still with you, I was telling you these things?

And you know what restrains him now [from being revealed]; it is so that he will be revealed at his own [appointed] time. For the mystery of lawlessness [rebellion against divine authority and the coming reign of lawlessness] is already at work; [but it is restrained] only until he who now restrains it is taken out of the way. Then the lawless one [the Antichrist] will be revealed and the Lord Jesus will slay him with the breath of His mouth and bring him to an end by the appearance of His coming. The coming of the [Antichrist, the lawless] one is through the activity of Satan, [attended] with great power [all kinds of counterfeit miracles] and [deceptive] signs and false wonders [all of them lies], and by unlimited seduction to evil and with all the deception of wickedness for those who are perishing, because they did not welcome the love of the truth [of the gospel] so as to be saved [they were spiritually blind, and rejected the truth that would have saved them]." 2 Thessalonians 2: 3-10.

I. They Manipulate Leaders to Destroy Nations

"Many political means well when they are running for the highest offices in the land, but once they win, they become targets of the forces of darkness who manipulate them to embrace corruption, greed and pride. Thus, they will begin to see themselves as mini gods and untouchables. Some Christians who go into politics often fall prey to satanic manipulation, because they become power hungry, and begin do human sacrifices, join cults, and other demonic fellowships to empower themselves. King Solomon started well, but ending up just like the ungodly king, which reflected in the lives of his children, even Rehoboam. Idol worship give Satan and his evil force power over the land. Manasseh was the opposite of Rehoboam, in his case, his father was good, but followed in that

blood line rehoboam, he perfected evil and celebrated wickedness.

Manasseh was twelve years old when he became king, and he reigned for fifty-five years in Jerusalem. But he did evil in the sight of the Lord, like the repulsive acts of the [pagan] nations whom the Lord dispossessed before the sons (descendants) of Israel. For he rebuilt the [idolatrous] high places which his father Hezekiah had torn down; and he set up altars for the Baals and made the Asherim and worshiped all the host of heaven [the sun, the moon, stars and planets] and served them. He built [pagan] altars in the house of the Lord, of which the Lord had said, "My Name shall be in Jerusalem forever." He built altars for all the host of heaven in the two courts of the house of the Lord. He made his sons pass through the fire [as an offering to his gods] in the Valley of Ben-hinnom; and he practiced witchcraft, used divination, and practiced sorcery, and dealt with mediums and spiritists. He did much evil in the sight of the Lord, provoking Him to anger.

Then he set the carved image of the idol which he had made in the house of God, of which God had said to David and to Solomon his son, "In this house and in Jerusalem, which I have chosen from all the tribes of Israel, I will put My Name [and the symbol of my Presence] forever; and I will not again remove Israel from the land which I appointed for your fathers, if they will only be careful to do everything that I have commanded them in regard to all the law, the statutes, and the ordinances given through Moses." So, Manasseh caused Judah and the inhabitants of Jerusalem to sin, by doing more evil than the [pagan] nations whom the Lord had destroyed before the sons of Israel." 2 Chronicles 33: 1-9.

J. They Partner with Mankind Against God

"Again, the word of the Lord came to me, saying, "Son of man, take up a dirge (funeral poem to be sung) for the king of

Tyre and say to him. Thus, says the Lord God, you had the full measure of perfection and finishing touch [of completeness], full of wisdom and perfect in beauty. "*You were in Eden, the garden of God; Every precious stone was your covering: The ruby, the topaz, and the diamond; The beryl, the onyx, and the jasper; The lapis lazuli, the turquoise, and the emerald; And the gold, the workmanship of your Settings, and your sockets, was in you. They were prepared on the day that you were created.* "*You were the anointed cherub who covers and protects, and I placed you there. You were on the holy mountain of God; You walked in the midst of the stones of fire [sparkling jewels].*

You were blameless in your ways from the day you were created until unrighteousness and evil were found in you. Through the abundance of your commerce, you were internally filled with lawlessness and violence, and you sinned; Therefore, I have cast you out as a profane and unholy thing from the mountain of God. And I have destroyed you, O covering cherub, from the midst of the stones of fire. "*Your heart was proud and arrogant because of your beauty; You destroyed your wisdom for the sake of your splendor. I cast you to the ground; I lay you before kings, that they might look at you.* "*You profaned your sanctuaries by the great quantity of your sins and the enormity of your guilt, by the unrighteousness of your trade. Therefore, I have brought forth a fire from your midst; It has consumed you, and I have reduced you to ashes on the earth in the sight of all who look at you.*"
Ezekiel 28 :11-18.

K. They Scatter Nations and Destroy Cities
Territorial spirits are experts in sowing seeds of discord, promoting racial disparities, and all forms of discrimination.

"Then I looked up, and saw four horns (powers)! So, I asked the angel who was speaking with me, "What are these?" And he answered me, "These are the horns [the powerful

*Gentile nations] that have scattered Judah (the Southern King-
dom), Israel (the Northern Kingdom), and Jerusalem (capital
city of Judah)." Then the Lord showed me four craftsmen. I
asked, "What are these [horns and craftsmen] coming to do?"
And he said, "These are the horns (powers) that have scattered
Judah so that no man raised up his head [because of the suffering inflicted by the Gentile nations]. But these craftsmen have
come to terrify them and make them panic, and throw down the
horns of the nations who have lifted up their horns against the
land of Judah in order to scatter it."* Zechariah 1: 18-21.

L. They Possess Non-Christian and Use them at Will

*"When He arrived at the other side in the country of the
Gadarenes, two demon-possessed men coming out of the tombs
met Him. They were so extremely fierce and violent that no one
could pass by that way. And a Canaanite woman from that
district came out and began to cry out [urgently], saying,
"Have mercy on me, O Lord, Son of David (Messiah); my
daughter is cruelly possessed by a demon."*
Matthew 8: 28; 15: 22.

Chapter 8

Babylonia Spirit Taking Over Territories

"By the rivers of Babylon, there we [captives] sat down and wept, when we remembered Zion [the city God imprinted on our hearts]." Psalm 137:1.

Today's Babylon is nothing compared to the old. Babylon was not a myth; it was a powerful kingdom. Today, Babylon is a type (typology) with historical, spiritual, and biblical significance. End time Babylon is spiritually, geographically, and methodically synonymous with greed, lust, wealth, power, intelligence, and pride, like today's America. America is the leading influence in satanism, sin, and worldliness today. Soon, Satanists (antichrists) will become lawmakers, power brokers, or even a president in the future. The Spirit of America corresponds historically and sociologically with the spirit of end-time Babylon both in real-time and futuristic terms.

Babylonia Spirit is the Queen of Darkness

"To the degree that she glorified herself and reveled and gloated in her sensuality [living deliciously and luxuriously], to that same degree impose on her torment and anguish, and mourning and grief; for in her heart she boasts, 'I sit as a queen [on a throne] and I am not a widow, and will never, ever see mourning or experience grief.' For this reason, in a single day her plagues (afflictions, calamities) will come, pestilence and mourning and famine, and she will be burned up with fire and completely consumed; for strong and powerful is the Lord God who judges her. "And the kings and political leaders of the earth, who committed immorality and lived luxuriously with her, will weep and beat their chests [in mourning] over her when they see the smoke of her burning, standing a long way

off, in fear of her torment, saying, 'Woe, woe, the great city, the strong city, Babylon! In a single hour your judgment has come.' And merchants of the earth will weep and grieve over her, because no one buys their cargo (goods, merchandise) anymore." Revelation 18:7-11.

Babylonia Spirits Feed on Christians

"Then one of the seven angels who had the seven bowls came and spoke with me, saying, "Come here, I will show you the judgment and doom of the great prostitute who is seated on many waters [influencing nations], she with whom the kings of the earth have committed acts of immorality, and the inhabitants of the earth have become intoxicated with the wine of her immorality." And the angel carried me away in the Spirit into a wilderness; and I saw a woman sitting on a scarlet beast that was entirely covered with blasphemous names, having seven heads and ten horns.

The woman was dressed in purple and scarlet, and adorned with gold, precious stones and pearls, [and she was] holding in her hand a gold cup full of the abominations and the filth of her [sexual] immorality. And on her forehead a name was written, a mystery: "Babylon the great, the mother of prostitutes (false religions, heresies) and of the abomination of the earth" I saw that the woman was drunk with the blood of the saints (God's people), and with the blood of the witnesses of Jesus [who were martyred]. When I saw her, I wondered in amazement." Revelation 17: 1-6.

Babylonia Spirit Will Make War against Christ and Us

"They will wage war against the Lamb (Christ), and the Lamb will triumph and conquer them, because He is Lord of lords and King of kings, and those who are with Him and on His side are the called and chosen (elect) and faithful." Then the angel said to me, "The waters which you saw, where the prostitute is seated, are peoples and multitudes and nations and

languages. And the ten horns which you saw, and the beast, these will hate the prostitute and will make her desolate and naked [stripped of her power and influence], and will eat her flesh and completely consume her with fire. For God has put it in their hearts to carry out His purpose by agreeing together to surrender their kingdom to the beast, until the [prophetic] words of God will be fulfilled. The woman whom you saw is the great city, which reigns over and dominates and controls the kings and the political leaders of the earth." Revelation 17: 14-18.

The Territory Called Miss Wickedness

"Then the heavy lead cover was lifted off the basket, and there was a woman sitting inside it. The angel said, "The woman's name is Wickedness," and he pushed her back into the basket and closed the heavy lid again. Then I looked up and saw two women flying toward us, gliding on the wind. They had wings like a stork, and they picked up the basket and flew into the sky. "Where are they taking the basket?" I asked the angel. He replied, "To the land of Babylonia, where they will build a temple for the basket. And when the temple is ready, they will set the basket there on its pedestal." Zechariah 5:7-11.

Don't Partner with Babylonia Spirits

"And he shouted with a mighty voice, saying, "Fallen, fallen [certainly to be destroyed] is Babylon the great! She has be-come a dwelling place for demons, a dungeon haunted by every unclean spirit, and a prison for every unclean and loathsome bird. For all the nations have drunk from the wine of the passion of her [sexual] immorality, and the kings and Political leaders of the earth have committed immorality with her, and the merchants of the earth have become rich by the wealth and economic power of her sensuous luxury." And I heard another voice from heaven, saying, "Come out of her, my people, so that you will not be a partner in her sins and receive her plagues." Revelation 18:2-4.

Past Babylon a Type of Tomorrow's Babylonia America

"Flee out of Babylon, let every one of you save his life! Do not be destroyed in her punishment, for this is the time of the Lord's vengeance; He is going to pay her what she has earned. Babylon has been a golden cup in the Lord's hand, intoxicating all the earth. The nations drank her wine; Therefore, the nations have gone mad. "And I will [completely] repay Babylon and all the people of Chaldea for all the evil that they have done in Zion—before your very eyes [I will do it]," says the Lord. "Behold, I am against you, O destroying mountain [conqueror of nations], who destroys the whole earth," declares the Lord, "I will stretch out My hand against you, and roll you down from the [rugged] cliffs, and will make you a burnt mountain (extinct volcano). "They will not take from you [even] a stone for a cornerstone nor any rock for a foundation, but you will be desolate forever," says the Lord. Lift up a signal in the land [to spread the news]! Blow the trumpet among the nations!

Dedicate the nations [for war] against her; Call against her the kingdoms of Ararat, Minni, and Ashkenaz. Appoint a marshal against her; Cause the horses to come up like bristly locusts [with their wings not yet released from their cases]. Prepare and dedicate the nations for war against her—The kings of Media, with their governors and commanders, and every land of their dominion. The land trembles and writhes [in pain and sorrow], for the purposes of the Lord against Babylon stand, to make the land of Babylon a desolation Without inhabitants. The mighty warriors of Babylon have ceased to fight; They remain in their strongholds. Their strength and power have failed; They are becoming [weak and helpless] like women. Their dwelling places are set on fire; The bars on her gates are broken. One courier runs to meet another, and one messenger to meet another, to tell the king of Babylon that his city has been captured from end to end; And that the fords [across the Euphrates] have been blocked and [the ferries] seized, and they have set the [great] marshes on fire, and the men of war are terrified. For thus says the Lord of hosts, the God of Israel:

"The Daughter of Babylon is like a threshing floor at the time it is being trampled and prepared; Yet in a little while the time of harvest will come for her. Nebuchadnezzar king of Babylon has devoured me, he has crushed me, he has set me down like an empty vessel. Like a monster he has swallowed me up, he has filled his belly with my delicacies; He has spit me out and washed me away. "May the violence done to me and to my flesh and blood be upon Babylon," The inhabitant of Zion will say; And, "May my blood be upon the inhabitants of Chaldea," Jerusalem will say. Therefore, thus says the Lord, "Behold, I will plead your case and take full vengeance for you; I will dry up her sea and great reservoir and make her fountain dry. Babylon will become a heap [of ruins], a haunt and dwelling place of jackals, an object of horror (an astonishing desolation) and a hissing [of scorn and amazement], without inhabitants. They (the Chaldean lords) will be roaring together [before their sudden capture] like young lions [roaring over their prey], they (the princes) will be growling like lions' cubs.

"When they are inflamed [with wine and lust during their drinking bouts], I will prepare them a feast [of My wrath] and make them drunk, that they may rejoice and may sleep a perpetual sleep and not wake up," declares the Lord. "I will bring them down like lambs to the slaughter, like rams together with male goats. "How Sheshak (Babylon) has been captured, and the praise of the whole earth been seized! How Babylon has become an astonishing desolation and an object of horror among the nations! "The sea has come up over Babylon; She has been engulfed with its tumultuous waves. "Her cities have become an astonishing desolation and an object of horror, a parched land and a desert, a land in which no one lives, and

through which no son of man passes. "I will punish and judge Bel [the handmade god] in Babylon and take out of his mouth what he has swallowed up [the stolen sacred articles and the captives of Judah and elsewhere].

The nations will no longer flow to him. Yes, the wall of Babylon has fallen down! "Come out of her midst, my people, and each of you [escape and] save yourself from the fierce anger of the Lord. "Now beware so that you do not lose heart, and so that you are not afraid at the rumor that will be heard in the land—For the rumor shall come one year, and after that another rumor in another year, and violence shall be in the land, ruler against ruler. "Therefore behold (listen carefully), the days are coming when I will judge and punish the idols of Babylon; Her whole land will be perplexed and shamed, and all her slain will fall in her midst. "Then heaven and earth and all that is in them will shout and sing for joy over Babylon, for the destroyers will come against her from the north," Says the Lord. Indeed, Babylon is to fall for the slain of Israel, as also for Babylon the slain of all the earth have fallen. You who have escaped the sword, Go away!

Do not stay! Remember the Lord from far away, and let [desolate] Jerusalem come into your mind. We are perplexed and ashamed, for we have heard reproach; Disgrace has covered our faces, for foreigners [from Babylon] have come into the [most] sacred parts of the sanctuary of the Lord [even those places forbidden to all but the appointed priest]. "Therefore be-hold, the days are coming," says the Lord, "When I will judge and punish the idols [of Babylon], and throughout her land the mortally wounded will groan." "Though Babylon should ascend to the heavens, and though she should fortify her lofty stronghold, yet destroyers will come on her from Me," says the Lord. The sound of an outcry [comes] from Babylon, and [the sound] of great destruction from the land of the Chaldeans! For the Lord is going to destroy Baby-

lon and make her a ruin, and He will still her great voice [that hums with city life]. And the waves [of her conquerors] roar like great waters, the noise of their voices is raised up [like the marching of an army].

For the destroyer is coming against her, against Babylon; And her mighty warriors will be captured, their bows are shattered; For the Lord is a God of [just] restitution; He will fully repay. "I will make her princes and her wise men drunk, her governors and her commanders and her mighty warriors; They will sleep a perpetual sleep and not wake up," Says the King—the Lord of hosts is His name. Thus, says the Lord of hosts, "The broad wall of Babylon will be completely overthrown, and the foundations razed, and her high gates will be set on fire; The peoples will labor in vain, and the nations become exhausted [only] for fire [that will destroy their work]." Jeremiah 51: 6-7, 24-58.

Chapter 9

Seven Territorial Realms Part 1

We are up against seven realms in both physical and spiritual warfare daily. New treatment apostles dealt with all seven realms and domains; they prevailed by the grace of God. I pray you will not go down or fall into the doom of failure or become a living dead. I pray you will not drown in the river of frustration or get overcome by the swamp of shame or reproach. I pray that God give you the grace to stand your ground and fight the good fight of faith to win on the day of battle, in Jesus' name.

1. The Terrestrial Realm: Land realm; powers of the land. Powers that are assigned to different areas in different communities. All the lands are divided accordingly and assigned geographically to territorial spirits, they network daily with other forces or territorial spirits in their various realms.

"There are also celestial bodies and ***terrestrial*** *bodies. The glory of the celestial is one, and the glory of the* ***terrestrial*** *is another." And the great dragon was thrown down, the age-old serpent who is called the devil and Satan, he who continually deceives and seduces the entire inhabited world; he was thrown down to the earth, and his angels were thrown down with him. Then I heard a loud voice in heaven, saying, now the salvation, and the power, and the kingdom (dominion, reign) of our God, and the authority of His Christ have come; for the accuser of our [believing] brothers and sisters has been thrown down [at last], he who accuses them and keeps bringing charges [of sinful behavior] against them before our God, day and night."* 1 Corinthians 15:40; Revelation 12:9-10.

2. The Celestial Realm: The sky realm; Powers of air.
"So, it will happen in that day that the LORD will visit and

punish the host (fallen angels) of heaven on high, and the kings of the earth on the earth. And you [He made alive when you] were [spiritually] dead and separated from Him because of your transgressions and sins, in which you once walked. You were following the ways of this world [influenced by this present age], in accordance with the prince of the power of the air (Satan), the spirit who is now at work in the disobedient [the unbelieving, who fight against the purposes of God]." Isaiah 24:21; Ephesians 2:1-3.

3. The Aquatic Realm: Water realm; Powers of the Sea, or what we often call: The marine spirit!

"Therefore rejoice, O heavens and you who dwell in them [in the presence of God]. Woe to the earth and the sea, because the devil has come down to you in great wrath, knowing that he has only a short time [remaining]!" And I heard every created thing that is in heaven or on earth or under the earth [in Hades, the realm of the dead] or on the sea, and everything that is in them, saying [together], "To Him who sits on the throne, and to the Lamb (Christ), be blessing and honor and glory and dominion forever and ever." Revelation 12:12; 5: 13.

"Daniel said, "I saw in my vision by night, and behold, the four winds of heaven were stirring up the great sea (the nations). And four great beasts, each different from the other, were coming up out of the sea [in succession]." Daniel 7:2-3.

4. The Heavenly Realm: Angelic Realm; Powers of the air.

"Lift up your eyes on high and see who has created these heavenly bodies, The One who brings out their host by number, He calls them all by name; Because of the greatness of His might and the strength of His power, not one is missing." Isaiah 40: 26.

There are Three Heavens according to Hebrews 7: 26. *"It was fitting for us to have such a High Priest [perfectly adapted to*

our needs], holy, blameless, unstained [by sin], separated from
sinners and exalted higher than the heavens. "

"Behold, the heavens and the highest of heavens belong to
the Lord your God, the earth and all that is in it. The heavens
are Yours; the earth also is Yours; The world and all that is in
it, You have founded and established them. "
Deuteronomy 10:14; Psalm 89: 11.

The First Heaven: This is beyond the visible sky our eyes can
see, the forces of darkness dwells here. The moon, stars, and
sun are housed there too, that is why nobody can shoot down
the moon, stars, or the sun.
"Then I saw a new heaven and a new earth; for the first
heaven and the first earth had passed away (vanished), and
there is no longer any sea. " Revelations 21: 1.

"He said to them, "I watched Satan fall from heaven like [a
flash of] lightning. " Luke 10:18.

"For the stars of heaven and their constellations will not
flash with their light; The sun will be dark when it rises, and the
moon will not shed its light. " Isaiah 13:10.

"And his tail swept [across the sky] and dragged away
*a **third** of the stars of **heaven** and flung them to the earth. And*
the dragon stood in front of the woman who was about to give
birth, so that when she gave birth, he might devour her child. "
Revelation 12:4.

"For our struggle is not against flesh and blood
[contending only with physical opponents], but against the
rulers, against the powers, against the world forces of this
[present] darkness, against the spiritual forces of wickedness
in the heavenly (supernatural) places. " Ephesians 6:12.

"There are also heavenly bodies [sun, moon and stars] and earthly bodies [humans, animals, and plants], but the glory and beauty of the heavenly is one kind, and the glory of the earthly is another. There is a glory and beauty of the sun, another glory of the moon, and yet another [distinctive] glory of the stars; and one star differs from another in glory and brilliance." 1 Corinthians 15: 40-41.

The Second or Mid-heaven: This is where God's Holy Angel are housed, the storage place where prayers are processed for delivery as answers.

"Then I looked, and I heard a solitary eagle flying in Mid-heaven [for all to see], saying with a loud voice, "Woe, woe, woe [great wrath is coming] to those who dwell on the earth, because of the remaining blasts of the trumpets which the three angels are about to sound [announcing ever greater judgments]!" Revelation 8:13.

Chapter 10

Seven Territorial Realms Part 2

"And there between the throne (with the four living creatures) and among the elders I saw a Lamb (Christ) standing, [bearing scars and wounds] as though it had been slain, with seven horns (complete power) and with seven eyes (complete know-ledge), which are the seven Spirits of God who have been sent [on duty] into all the earth." Revelation 5:6.

The Third Heaven: This is the throne of Grace, the city of gold where Jesus is the Sun. *"And there will no longer be night; they have no need for lamplight or sunlight, because the Lord God will illumine them; and they will reign [as kings] forever and ever. I know a man in Christ who fourteen years ago—whether in the body I do not know, or out of the body I do not know, [only] God knows—such a man was caught up to the third heaven."* Revelation 22:5; 2 Corinthians 12:2.

"Then I saw a new heaven and a new earth; for the first heaven and the first earth had passed away (vanished), and there is no longer any sea. And I saw the holy city, new Jerusalem, coming down out of heaven from God, arrayed like a bride adorned for her husband; and then I heard a loud voice from the throne, saying, "See! The tabernacle of God is among men, and He will live among them, and they will be His people, and God Himself will be with them [as their God,] and He will wipe away every tear from their eyes; and there will no longer be death; there will no longer be sorrow and anguish, or crying, or pain; for the former order of things has passed away." And He who sits on the throne said, "Behold, I am making all things new." Also, He said, "Write, for these words

are faithful and true [they are accurate, incorruptible, and trustworthy]."

I saw no temple in it, for the Lord God Almighty [the Omnipotent, the Ruler of all] and the Lamb are its temple. And the city has no need of the sun nor of the moon to give light to it, for the glory (splendor, radiance) of God has illumined it, and the Lamb is its lamp and light. The nations [the redeemed people from the earth] will walk by its light, and the kings of the earth will bring into it their glory. By day (for there will be no night there) its gates will never be closed [in fear of evil]; and they will bring the glory (splendor, majesty) and the honor of the nations into it; and nothing that defiles or profanes or is unwashed will ever enter it, nor anyone who practices abominations [detestable, morally repugnant things] and lying, but only those [will be admitted] whose names have been written in the Lamb's Book of Life." Revelation 21: 1-5, 22-27.

*"Blessed and worthy of praise be the God and Father of our Lord Jesus Christ, who has blessed us with every spiritual blessing in the heavenly **realms** in Christ."* Ephesians 1:3.

5. The Hellish Realm: Shoel or Hades realm; Powers of Hell.
*"Then He will say to those on His left, 'Leave Me, you cursed ones, into the eternal fire which has been prepared for the devil and his angels (demons); Then these [unbelieving people] will go away into eternal (unending) punishment, but those who are righteous and in right standing with God [will go, by His remarkable grace]into eternal (unending) life Then death and Hades [the **realm** of the dead] were thrown into the lake of fire. This is the second death, the lake of fire [the eternal separation from God]."* Matthew 25: 41, 46; Revelation 20:14.

The Rich Man in Hell: *"And he cried out, 'Father Abraham, have mercy on me, and send Lazarus so that he may dip the tip of his finger in water and cool my tongue, because I am in* *severe agony in this flame. But Abraham said, Son, remember that in your lifetime you received your good things [all the comforts and delights], and Lazarus likewise bad things [all the discomforts and dis-tresses]; but now he is comforted here [in paradise], while you are in severe agony. And besides all this, between us and you [people] a great chasm has been fixed, so that those who want to come over from here to you will not be able, and none may cross over from there to us.'*

So, the rich man said, 'Then, father [Abraham], I beg you to send Lazarus to my father's house—for I have five brothers—in order that he may solemnly warn them and witness to them, so that they too will not come to this place of torment.' But Abraham said, 'They have [the Scriptures given by] Moses and the [writings of the] Prophets; let them listen to them.' He replied, 'No, father Abraham, but if someone from the dead goes to them, they will repent [they will change their old way of thinking and seek God and His righteousness].' And he said to him, 'If they do not listen to [the messages of] Moses and the Prophets, they will not be persuaded even if someone rises from the dead.'" Luke 16: 24-31.

*"Therefore Sheol (the **realm** of the dead) has increased its appetite and opened its mouth beyond measure; And Jerusalem's splendor, her multitude, her [boisterous] uproar and her [drunken] revelers descend into it."* Isaiah 5:14.

6. The Realm of the Flesh: The carnal realm; The Power of the mind and heart.

*"We know that the Law is spiritual, but I am a creature of the **flesh** [worldly, self-reliant—carnal and unspiritual], sold into slavery to sin [and serving under its control]. For I know that nothing good lives in me, that is, in my flesh [my human nature, my worldliness—my sinful capacity]. For the willingness [to do good] is present in me, but the doing of good is not. For from within, [that is] out the heart of men, come base and*

malevolent thoughts and schemes, acts of sexual immorality, thefts, murders, adulteries, acts of greed and Covetousness, wicked-ness, deceit, unrestrained conduct, envy and jealousy, slander and profanity, arrogance and self-righteous-ness and foolish-ness (poor judgment). All these evil things [schemes and desires] come from within and defile and dishonor the man." Romans 7:14, 18; Mark 7:21-23.

For though we walk in the flesh [as mortal men], we are not carrying on our [spiritual] warfare according to the flesh and using the weapons of man. The weapons of our warfare are not physical [weapons of flesh and blood]. Our weapons are divinely powerful for the destruction of fortresses. We are destroying sophisticated arguments and every exalted and proud thing that sets itself up against the [true] knowledge of God, and we are taking every thought and Purpose captive to the obedience of Christ." 2 Corinthians 10:3-5.

The Big Question for You and Me
*The sinners in Zion are terrified; Trembling has seized the god-less. [They cry] "Who among us can live with the consuming **fire**? Who among us can live with **everlasting** burning?"* Isaiah 33:14.

The Way to Victory Over the Power of the Flesh
*But clothe yourselves with the Lord Jesus Christ, and make no provision for [nor even think about gratifying] the **flesh** in regard to its improper desires. I have been crucified with Christ [that is, in Him I have shared His crucifixion]; it is no longer I who live, but Christ lives in me. The life I now live in the body I live by faith [by adhering to, relying on, and completely trusting] in the Son of God, who loved me and gave Himself up for me."* Romans 13:14; Galatians 2:20.

7. **The Spirit Realm:** The unseen realm, the places, and the life you live in the dream when you sleep.

"However, you are not [living] in the flesh [controlled by the sinful nature] but in the Spirit, if in fact the Spirit of God lives in you [directing and guiding you]. But if anyone does not have the Spirit of Christ, he does not belong to Him [and is not a child of God]. If Christ lives in you, though your [natural] body is dead because of sin, your spirit is alive because of righteousness [which He provides]. And if the Spirit of Him who raised Jesus from the dead lives in you, He who raised Christ Jesus from the dead will also give life to your mortal bodies through His Spirit, who lives in you." Romans 8:9-11.

You and I Can Oversee All Realms in Christ

"And He put all things [in every realm] in subjection under Christ's feet, and appointed Him as [supreme and authoritative] head over all things in the church, which is His body, the fullness of Him who fills and completes all things in all [believers]." Ephesians 1: 22-23.

Although God have given us power to oversee all realms in Christ. We must not allow our carelessness, recklessness, and complacency to serve as pathways, doorways, and entering points, for territorial spirits to hinder us, or hold us captive, and truncate our goals/plans.

FIGHT FOR YOUR TERRITORY

Chapter 11

How We Can Be Your Own Enemy

"Whoever is partner with a thief hates his own life; He hears the curse [when swearing an oath to testify], but discloses no-thing [and commits perjury by omission]. The fear of man brings a snare, but whoever trusts in and puts his confidence in the Lord will be exalted and safe. For I know that nothing good lives in me, that is, in my flesh [my human nature, my worldliness—my sinful capacity]. For the willingness [to do good] is present in me, but the doing of good is not. But if I am doing the very thing I do not want to do, I am no longer the one doing it [that is, it is not me that acts], but the sin [nature] which lives in me. So, I find it to be the law [of my inner self], that evil is present in me, the one who wants to do good."
Proverbs 29:24-25; Romans 7:18, 20-21.

1. When God is Not First in Our Lives: *"Adulterers and adulteresses! Do you not know that friendship with the world is enmity with God? Whoever therefore wants to be a friend of the world makes himself an enemy of God."* James 4:4.

2.When We Reject Good, We Settle to Bad: *"Israel has rejected the good; The enemy will pursue him."* Hosea 8: 3.

3. When We Value Men More Than God: *"My people are destroyed for lack of knowledge. Because you have rejected knowledge, I also will reject you from being priest for Me; Because you have forgotten the law of your God, I also will forget your children."* Hosea 4:6.

4. When Our Flesh Leads Instead of God's Spirit: *"I do not do the good I want, but the evil I do not want is what I keep on* *doing. Wretched man that I am! Who will deliver me from this body of death." Rom 7:19, 24.*

5. When We Fight and Resist God's Legitimate Leaders:

"Therefore, whoever resists the authority resists the ordinance of God, and those who resist will bring judgment on themselves." Romans 13:2.

6. When We Are Proud and Refuse to humble Ourselves:

"But He gives more grace. Therefore, He says: "God resists the proud, but gives grace to the humble."
James 4: 6.

7. When We Work Evil Against Each Other: *"Oh, that my head were waters and my eyes a fountain of tears, that I might weep day and night for the slain of the daughter of my people! Oh, that I had in the wilderness a lodging place (a mere shelter) for wayfaring men, that I might leave my people and go away from them! For they are all adulterers [worship-ping idols instead of the Lord], [They are] an assembly of treacherous men [of weak character, men without integrity]. "They bend their tongue like their bow; [Their] lies and not truth prevail and grow strong in the land; For they proceed from evil to evil, and they do not know and understand and acknowledge Me," says the Lord. Let everyone beware of his neighbor and do not trust any brother. For every brother is a supplanter [like Jacob, a deceiver, ready to grab his brother's heel], and every neighbor goes around as a slanderer.*

"Everyone deceives and mocks his neighbor and does not speak the truth. They have taught their tongue to speak lies; They exhaust themselves with sin and cruelty. "Your dwelling is in the midst of deceit [oppression upon oppression and deceit upon deceit]; Through deceit they refuse to know (understand) Me," says the Lord. Therefore, thus says the Lord of hosts, "Behold, I will refine them [through suffering] and test them;

For how else should I deal with the daughter of My people? "Their tongue is a murderous arrow; It speaks deceit; With his mouth one speaks peace to his neighbor, but in his heart he lays traps and waits in ambush for him. "Shall I not punish them for these things?" says the Lord. "Shall I not avenge Myself on such a nation as this?" Jeremiah 9: 1-9.

8. When We Become Instrument of Confusion: *"I urge you, brothers, and sisters, to keep your eyes on those who cause dissensions and create obstacles or introduce temp-tations [for others] to commit sin, [acting in ways] contrary to the doctrine which you have learned. Turn away from them. For such people do not serve our Lord Christ, but their own appetites and base desires. By smooth and flattering speech they deceive the hearts of the unsuspecting [the innocent and the naive]. O Lord, to us belong confusion and open shame—to our kings, to our princes, and to our fathers—because we have sinned against You. Again, I say to you, that if two believers on earth agree [that is, are of one mind, in harmony] about anything that they ask [within the will of God], it will be done for them by My Father in heaven. Behold, how good and how pleasant it is for brothers to dwell together in unity! It is like the dew of [Mount] Hermon coming down on the hills of Zion; For there the Lord has commanded the blessing: life forevermore."*
Romans 16: 17-18; Daniel 9:8. Matthew 18: 9; Psalm 133: 1, 3.

9. When We Refuse to Forgive: *"For if you forgive others their trespasses [their reckless and willful sins], your heavenly Father will also forgive you. But if you do not forgive others [nurturing your hurt and anger with the result that it interferes with your relationship with God], then your Father will not forgive your trespasses. "For I wrote to you out of great distress and with an anguished heart, and with many tears, not to cause you sorrow but to make you realize the [overflowing] love which I have especially for you."* Matthew 6: 14-15.

"You have heard that it was said to the men of old, 'You shall not murder,' and 'Whoever murders shall be guilty before the court.' But I say to you that everyone who continues to be angry with his brother or harbors malice against him shall be guilty before the court; and whoever speaks [contemptuously and insultingly] to his brother, Raca (You empty-headed idiot), shall be guilty before the supreme court (Sanhedrin); and whoever says, 'You fool!' shall be in danger of the fiery hell. So, if you are presenting your offering at the altar, and while there you remember that your brother has something [such as a grievance or legitimate complaint] against you, leave your offering there at the altar and go. First make peace with your brother, and then come and present your offering."
Matthew 5: 21-24.

"But if someone has caused [all this] sorrow, he has caused it not to me, but in some degree—not to put it too severely—[he has distressed and grieved] all of you. For such a one this punishment by the majority is sufficient, so instead [of further rebuke, now] you should rather [graciously] forgive and comfort and encourage him, to keep him from being overwhelmed by excessive sorrow. Therefore, I urge you to reinstate him in your affections and reaffirm your love for him. For this was my purpose in writing, to see if you would stand the test, whether you are obedient and committed to following my instruction in all things.

If you forgive anyone anything, I too forgive [that one]; and what I have forgiven, if I have forgiven anything, has been for your sake in the presence of [and with the approval of] Christ, to keep Satan from taking advantage of us; for we are not ignorant of his schemes."
2 Corinthians 2: 5-11.

10. When We Refuse to Resist Satan and Submit to God: *"Therefore, submit to God. Resist the devil and he will flee from you."* James 4:7.

We Can Do Real Damage to Our Own Lives

There is no doubt that you and I can be our own territorial enemies of joy, progress, and breakthrough, because we sometimes give the devil the ammunition to use against us. *"All things are lawful [that is, morally legitimate, permissible], but not all things are beneficial or advantageous. All things are lawful, but not all things are constructive [to character] and edifying [to spiritual life]."* 1 Corinthians 10:23.

Ways We Can Become Our Own Enemies

Our carelessness and recklessness can serve as doorways and entering points that territorial spirits can use to hinder us or hold us captive and truncate our goals/plans as fellows below:

1. **Careless Words:** We can use words to create good or bad life experiences or occurrences for ourselves. Life and death are in the power of our tongues.
2. **Careless Spending:** You cannot eat your cake and have it too. There is nothing good about being in the bondage of debt. A borrower will always be a slave to the lender.
3. **Careless Decisions:** Our decisions can make or break us. One bad decision can cause the pain of a lifetime.
4. **Careless Investments:** I learned this vital life lesson in a very hard and bad way. When poverty and debt come knocking at the door of your life, shame, and reproach are not far away.
5. **Laziness:** It is a disease and leads to the temptation of criminal intentions. Laziness makes people fall for evil attracttions and embrace criminality as a profession.
6. **Selfishness:** It is the mother of all sins. It gave birth to greed, pride, and strife. Selfishness is married to lust; together, they can turn a beautiful home into a home of pain, bitterness, and shame.
7. **Walking in the Flesh:** When you walk in the flesh, you will reap the fruits of the flesh. Sometimes we place great value on

things (gold, diamonds, and silver) and animals (pets); more than we do underprivileged fellow humans.

8. **Corruption:** Beware of the love of money, materialism, and fame. Together they constitute the tree of all evil. The tree of corruption thrives on the soil of greed, lust, and pride.

9. **Curses:** They are powerful instruments of destruction; a cursed person will not enjoy life's goodness until the curse is removed. A curse can turn a king into a slave in due time.

10. **Evil Covenants:** These are deadly by design. Any agreement in part or partnership with the devil, directly or indirectly and will always impair joy.

11. **When You Place Yourself First and God Last in Your Life:** You cannot live alone with the life God has given you. When you put God last, your life will begin to work in reverse, and against the divine order of life.

12. **Lack of Integrity:** It almost impossible to go far in life, if nobody can trust you. Integrity attracts favor and blessings.

13. **Prayerlessness:** If we fail to pray, we fall and become prey to the forces of darkness—*Territorial Spirits.*

14. **Sowing Bad Seeds:** The Bible is noticeably clear on this, we reap whatever we sow with interest, good or bad.

Territorial Spirits Prevail if We Are Our Own Enemies

"For these things I weep; My eye, my eye overflows with water; Because the comforter, who should restore my life, Is far from me. My children are desolate Because the enemy prevailed." Lamentations 1:16.

What Then Can We Do, How Can We Fix This Problem?

*"But **seek first** the kingdom of God and His righteousness, and all these things shall be added to you." "The one who loves and unselfishly seeks the best for his [believing] brother lives in the Light, and in him there is no occasion for stumbling or offense [he does not hurt the cause of Christ or lead others to sin]."* Matthew 6:33; 1 John 2:10.

74

Chapter 12

Victory Over Territorial Spirits Part 1

"They will be like mighty men Trampling down their enemies in the mire of the streets in the battle; And they will fight because the Lord is with them, And the [enemies'] riders on horses will be shamed." Zechariah 10:5.

We Must Fight the Good Fight of Faith, or We Go Astray

For us to be able to possess our territories, we must be ready to war and battle the forces of darkness who are daily contending to steal all that God has given to us in Christ Jesus.

"Fight the good fight of the faith [in the conflict with evil]; take hold of the eternal life to which you were called, and [for which] you made the good confession [of faith] in the presence of many witnesses. O Timothy, guard and keep safe the deposit [of godly truth] entrusted to you, turn away from worldly and godless chatter [with its profane, empty words], and the contradictions of what is falsely called "knowledge"— which some have professed and by doing so have erred (missed the mark) and strayed from the faith." 1 Timothy 6:12, 20-21.

When We Go Astray, Satan Can Afflict Us

The devil rejoices when you and I stray away from the truth of God's word, become deceived, frustrated, and discouraged. God has given us the power to bind territorial spirits when they trouble. We could also bind ourselves (or their become lawful captives) when we create problems for ourselves. We could become our own hinderance because of our inaction or over-reaction; poor decisions and choices; lust and greed; pride and anger. Territorial spirits often seek subtle ways to exploit and maximize our division; individuality, disabilities, inabilities, and irresponsibility to steal, kill and destroy our homes and hinder us from fulfilling the great commission. *"Before I was afflicted, I went astray, but now I keep and honor Your word [with loving obedience]."* Psalm 119: 67.

Sin Weakens Us and Makes Us Slaves

Prophet Eli's children did not have the fear of God, they were afraid of lack and hunger. Thus, they live to serve their belly and money, not God. They added sin to sin, greed, lust, pride, and immorality. They were slaves to their emotions which made them desecrate their priestly offices. At the end, they ended up in shame, they were both captured, held captive, and killed like ordinary men not as princes. No wonder the Bible says in Romans 6:23 that: *"The wages of Sin is death."* If you don't put your ways right with God, I pray you will not regret it like the children of Eli who enjoyed temporal fun at the expense of their relationship with God and eternal glory.

"So, it happened that as the ark of the covenant of the Lord came into the camp, all [the people of] Israel shouted with a great shout, and the earth resounded. When the Philistines heard the noise of the shout, they said, "What does the noise of this great shout in the camp of the Hebrews mean?" Then they understood that the ark of the Lord had come into the camp. The Philistines were afraid, for they said, "God has come into the camp." And they said, "Woe [disaster is coming] to us! For nothing like this has happened before. Woe to us! Who will rescue us from the hand of these mighty gods? These are the gods who struck the Egyptians with all kinds of plagues in the wilderness. Take courage, and be men, O Philistines, so that you do not become servants to the Hebrews, as they have been servants to you; act like men and fight!" So, the Philistines fought; Israel was defeated, and every man fled to his tent. It was a very great defeat, for thirty-thousand foot soldiers of Israel fell. Also, the ark of God was taken; and the two sons of Eli, Hophni and Phinehas, were killed." 1 Samuel 4: 5-11.

How to Be Victorious Over Territorial Spirits

1. **You must be truly born again:** It is too dangerous not to be born again according to 2 Timothy 2:26 *"And that they may recover themselves out of the snare of the devil, who are taken captive by him at his will." If you are not born again, they devil can take you captive and slaughter you at will any day he chooses.*

There are some of us that are not truly born again according to 1 John 2:19. *"They went out from us [seeming at first to be Christians], but they were not really of us [because they were not truly born again, and spiritually transformed]; for if they had been of us, they would have remained with us; but they went out [teaching false doctrine], so that it would be clearly shown that none of them are of us."*

Your Hands Must Be Clean

It is not good for you to claim to be born again, but then become a burden to the body of Christ through your way of living. Or become an instrument of destruction in Satan's hands to cause confusion, distraction, and division. Are you really born again, or are you a pretender? If you are a pretender, I may not know who you are on the inside, but God knows, God does not have any respect for pretenders.

"Do not be deceived, God is not mocked [He will not allow Himself to be ridiculed, nor treated with contempt nor allow His precepts to be scornfully set aside]; for whatever a man sows, this and this only is what he will reap. For the one who sows to his flesh [his sinful capacity, his worldliness, his disgraceful impulses] will reap from the flesh ruin and destruction, but the one who sows to the Spirit will from the Spirit reap eternal life. "Behold, the Lord's hand is not so short that it cannot save, nor His ear so impaired That it cannot hear. But your wickedness has separated you from your God, and your sins have hidden His face from you so that He does not hear.

For your hands are defiled with blood and your fingers with wickedness [with sin, with injustice, with wrongdoing]; Your lips have spoken lies, Your tongue mutters wickedness. No one sues righteously [but for the sake of doing injury to others— to take some undue advantage], and no one pleads [his case] in truth; [but rather] They trust in empty arguments and speak lies; They conceive trouble and bring forth injustice."
Galatians 6: 7-8 and Isaiah 59: 1-4.

Nothing Should Separate You from Christ's Love

Satan's passion is to separate you and me from God's word, way, and from Christ's love. He wants to isolate you and then destroy you. Don't allow anything or anyone to separate you from God's love, protection, and favor.

"Who shall ever separate us from the love of Christ? Will tribulation, or distress, or persecution, or famine, or nakedness, or danger, or sword? Just as it is written and forever remains written, "FOR YOUR SAKE WE ARE PUT TO DEATH ALL DAY LONG; WE ARE REGARDED AS SHEEP FOR THE SLAUGHTER." Yet in all these things we are more than conquerors and gain an over-whelming victory through Him who loved us [so much that He died for us]. For I am convinced [and continue to be convinced—beyond any doubt] that neither death, nor life, nor angels, nor principalities, nor things present and threatening, nor things to come, nor powers, nor height, nor depth, nor any other created thing, will be able to separate us from the [unlimited] love of God, which is in Christ Jesus our Lord."
Romans 8: 35-39.

Know Who You Are in Christ

You are not a toy, or a loser, and you are not a failure. Stop selling your positive choices for cookies. Stop trading or giving away your success for soups, or important life decisions for desserts. You were created for a purpose; you are not a waste. You are God's workmanship according to Ephesians 2: 10. *"For we are His workmanship [His own master work, a work of art], created in Christ Jesus [reborn from above—spiritually transformed, renewed, ready to be used] for good works, which God prepared [for us] beforehand [taking paths which He set], so that we would walk in them [living the good life which He prearranged and made ready for us]."*

I encourage you to be content with what you have, so you don't give place to greed or the devil. God knows your needs. He will not let you down if you can truly trust and wait on Him according to Hebrews 13: 5. *"Let your character [your moral essence, your inner nature] be free from the love of money [shun greed—be financially ethical], being content with what you have; for He has said, "I will never [under any circumstances] desert you [nor give you up nor leave you without support, nor will I in any degree leave you helpless], nor will I forsake or let you down or relax My hold on you [assuredly not]!"*

Be Watchful and Be Prayerful

Prayer changes things when we pray with sincerity and faith. Where man's ability ends are where God's enduring possibilities begins. Where man's capacity fails, is where God's capability begins. The joy we have as Christians is that God's grace, love, and mercies are made perfect in our weaknesses. Prayer can do what God can do, that is why He asked us to pray. When we pray, we are submitting to His power, grace, and will. Pray works if we can work it by faith, submission, and patience.

"Therefore, humble yourselves under the mighty hand of God [set aside self-righteous pride], so that He may exalt you [to a place of honor in His service] at the appropriate time, casting all your cares [all your anxieties, all your worries, and all your concerns, once and for all] on Him, for He cares about you [with deepest affection, and watches over you very carefully]. Be sober [well balanced and self-disciplined], be alert and cautious at all times. That enemy of yours, the devil,

prowls around like a roaring lion [fiercely hungry], seeking someone to devour. But resist him, be firm in your faith [against his attack—rooted, established, immovable], knowing that the same experiences of suffering are being experienced by your brothers and sisters throughout the world. [You do not suffer alone.]" 1 Peter 5: 6-9.

Prayer Is Warfare as We Exercise Our God Given Power

God has given us the power to bind and lose according to His word and will by His Spirit. Jesus taught us that before we can recover our blessings from the strong man— [Territorial spirits or their agents], stole from us, we must first bind the strong man— [Territorial spirits or their agents]. I like the way the *Amplified Holy Bible* expressed the word bound as whatever you allow or forbids, when you bind and lose, which means, God put you in charge, because Jesus has restored your dominion when He said; Behold, I give you power!

"I assure you and most solemnly say to you, whatever you bind [forbid, declare to be improper and unlawful] on earth shall have [already] been bound in heaven, and whatever you loose [permit, declare lawful] on earth shall have [already] been loosed in heaven. But if it is by the Spirit of God that I cast out the demons, then the kingdom of God has come upon you [before you expected it]. Or how can anyone go into a strong man's house and steal his property unless he first overpowers and ties up the strong man? Then he will ransack and rob his house. Listen carefully: I have given you authority [that you now possess] to tread on serpents and scorpions, and [the ability to exercise authority] over all the power of the enemy (Satan); and nothing will [in any way] harm you."
Matthew 18:18-19; 12: 28-29; Luke 10: 19.

Chapter 13

Victory Over Territorial Spirits Part 2

"For You have encircled me with strength for the battle; You have subdued under me those who rose up against me." Psalm 18:39.

Do Not Give Territorial Spirits Permission to Operate

Sometimes we are the ones who fail to be watchmen over our territories. In other words, we permit territorial spirits activities in our homes, communities, and cities. In his own time, the prophet Habakkuk was concerned about the activities of the territorial spirits in the land. Some of us have left our God-given assigned position or territory because of greed and impatience to seek and serve the god of mammon (Money). Many have turned away from the call of God to serve tables, and others have left their original call of God to become prophets and media evangelists, where they can deceive to accumulate earthly wealth through con games. Satan demanded permission to shake and attack Peter, Jesus prayed for him, but Peter did nothing. Peter became a backslider. Were it not for God's mercies, he would have turned his back on God.

"I will stand at my guard post and station myself on the tower; And I will keep watch to see what He will say to me, and what answer I will give [as His spokesman] when I am reproved." Habakkuk 2: 1.

"Simon, Simon (Peter), listen! Satan has demanded Permission to sift [all of] you like grain; but I have prayed [especially] for you [Peter], that your faith [and confidence in Me] may not fail; and you, once you have turned back again [to Me], stren-gthen and support your brothers [in the faith]."

And Peter said to Him, "Lord, I am ready to go with You both to prison and to death!" Jesus said, "I say to you, Peter, before the rooster crows today, you will [utterly] deny three times that you know Me. Then they seized Him, and led Him away and brought Him to the [elegant] house of the [Jewish] high priest.

And Peter was following at a [safe] distance. After they had kindled a fire in the middle of the courtyard and had sat down together, Peter sat among them. And a servant-girl, seeing him as he sat in the firelight and looking intently at him, said, "This man was with Him too." But Peter denied it, saying, "Woman, I do not know Him!" A little later someone else saw him and said, "You are one of them too." But Peter said, "Man, I am not!" After about an hour had passed, another man began to insist, "This man was with Him, for he is a Galilean too." But Peter said, "Man, I do not know what you are talking about." Immediately, while he was still speaking, a rooster crowed. The Lord turned and looked at Peter. And Peter remembered the word of the Lord, how He had told him, "Before a rooster crows today, you will deny Me three times." And he went out and wept bitterly [deeply grieved and distressed]."
Luke 22: 31-34; 54-62.

Delight Yourself in the Lord and In His Word

"Now yield and submit yourself to Him [agree with God and be conformed to His will] and be at peace; In this way [you will prosper and great] good will come to you. "Please receive the law and instruction from His mouth and establish His words in your heart and keep them. "If you return to the Almighty [and submit and humble yourself before Him], you will be built up [and restored]; If you remove unrighteousness far from your tents, and place your gold in the dust, and the gold of Ophir among the stones of the brooks [considering it of little value], and make the Almighty your gold and your precious silver, then you will have delight in the Almighty, and you will lift up your face to God. "You will pray to Him, and He will hear you,

And you will pay your vows. "You will also decide and decree a thing, and it will be established for you; and the light [of God's favor] will shine upon your ways." Job 22: 21-28.

Beware of False Prophets, Preachers, and Teachers

"Beware of the false prophets, [teachers] who come to you dressed as sheep [appearing gentle and innocent], but inwardly are ravenous wolves. By their fruit you will recognize them [that is, by their contrived doctrine and self-focus]. Do people pick grapes from thorn bushes or figs from thistles? Even so, every healthy tree bears good fruit, but the unhealthy tree bears bad fruit. A good tree cannot bear bad fruit, nor can a bad tree bear good fruit. Every tree that does not bear good fruit is cut down and thrown into the fire. Therefore, by their fruit you will recognize them [as false prophets]. "Not everyone who says to Me, 'Lord, Lord,' will enter the kingdom of heaven, but only he who does the will of My Father who is in heaven." For false Christs and false prophets will appear and they will provide great signs and wonders, so as to deceive, if possible, even the elect (God's chosen ones). Listen carefully, I have told you in advance. So, if they say to you, 'Look! He is in the wilderness,' do not go out there, or, 'Look! He is in the inner rooms [of a house],' do not believe it. For just as the lightning comes from the east and flashes as far as the west, so will be the coming [in glory] of the Son of Man [everyone will see Him clearly]. Wherever the corpse is, there the vultures will flock together." Matthew 7:15-21; 24: 24-27.

Put on the Whole Armor of God

"In conclusion, be strong in the Lord [draw your strength from Him and be empowered through your union with Him] and in the power of His [boundless] might. Put on the full armor of God [for His precepts are like the splendid armor of a heavily-armed soldier], so that you may be able to [successfully] stand up against all the schemes and the strategies and the deceits of the devil. For our struggle is not against flesh and blood [con-

tending only with physical opponents], but against the rulers, against the powers, against the world forces of this [present] darkness, against the spiritual forces of wickedness in the heavenly (supernatural) places. Therefore, put on the complete armor of God, so that you will be able to [successfully] resist and stand your ground in the evil day [of danger], and having done everything [that the crisis demands], to stand firm [in your place, fully prepared, immovable, victorious].

So, stand firm and hold your ground, having tightened the wide band of truth (personal integrity, moral courage) around your waist and having put on the breastplate of righteousness (an upright heart), and having strapped on your feet the gospel of peace in preparation [to face the enemy with firm-footed stability and the readiness produced by the good news]. Above all, lift up the [protective] shield of faith with which you can extinguish all the flaming arrows of the evil one. And take the helmet of salvation, and the sword of the Spirit, which is the Word of God. With all prayer and petition pray [with specific requests] at all times [on every occasion and in every season] in the Spirit, and with this in view, stay alert with all per-severance and petition [interceding in prayer] for all God's people." Ephesians 6: 10-18.

Don't Be Deceived, Be Careful

"Let no one cheat you of your reward, taking delight in false humility and worship of angels, intruding into those things which he has not seen, vainly puffed up by his fleshly mind, and not holding fast to the Head, from whom all the body, nourished and knit together by joints and ligaments, grows with the increase that is from God. Therefore, if you died with Christ from the basic principles of the world, why, as though living in the world, do you subject yourselves to regulations— "Do not touch, do not taste, do not handle," which all concern things which perish with the using—according to the commandments

and doctrines of men? These things indeed have an appearance of wisdom in self-imposed religion, false humility, and neglect of the body, but are of no value against the indulgence of the flesh." Colossians 2: 18-21.

We Must All Fight, Don't Shy Away, Get in the Fight

People everywhere are fighting to preserve their territories and exercise their God-given dominion to protect what is theirs. The exact process applies in the spiritual realm. So, I encourage you, my friend, not to shy away; wear your fighting gloves and get in the fight. Fight the good fight of faith. Every one of us has a promised land we must fight to possess. Please, wear your Christ army armor and let us fight to win.

"Behold, I am with you and will keep [careful watch over you and guard] you wherever you may go, and I will bring you back to this [promised] land; for I will not leave you until I have done what I have promised you." Genesis 28:15.

God's Angels Are Fighting Daily to Get to Our Territory

When you and I pray for blessings, protection, favor, and healing, territorial spirits fight to hinder our answered prayer requests from reaching us and manifesting in the physical realm. Such was the case of Daniel, Daniel was seeking the face of God for understanding, but the territorial spirits in charge of the kingdom of Persia fought against God's angel trying to bring the answer to Daniel's prayer into physical manifestation. God helped the angel with reinforcement; thus, he was able to deliver the answer to Daniel's prayer. Who knows if the reason you have not received your answer is because of the territorial spirits in charge of your village, town, community, or city? Our prayer helps the angels break through satanic strongholds to bring answers to us. If you don't fight in the place of prayer, the answers to your prayers may be delayed.

"Then behold, a hand touched me and set me unsteadily on my hands and knees. So, he said to me, "O Daniel, you highly

regarded and greatly beloved man, understand the words that I am about to say to you and stand upright, for I have now been sent to you." And while he was saying this word to me, I stood up trembling.

Then he said to me, "Do not be afraid, Daniel, for from the first day that you set your heart on understanding this and on humbling yourself before your God, your words were heard, and I have come in response to your words. But the prince of the kingdom of Persia was standing in opposition to me for twenty-one days. Then, behold, Michael, one of the chief [of the celestial] princes, came to help me, for I had been left there with the kings of Persia. Now I have come to make you understand what will happen to your people in the latter days, for the vision is in regard to the days yet to come." Then he said, "Do you understand [fully] why I came to you? Now I shall return to fight against the [hostile] prince of Persia; and when I have gone, behold, the prince of Greece is about to come."
Daniel 4: 10-14, 20.

Chapter 14

Bringing Down Territorial Altars

"Keep actively watching and praying that you may not come into temptation; the spirit is willing, but the body is weak. He went away a second time and prayed, saying, "My Father, if this cannot pass away unless I drink it, Your will be done." Matthew 26:41-42.

1. We have a responsibility to destroy the high places of evil according to Deuteronomy 12: 2-3; and 33:29. *"You shall utterly destroy all the places where the nations whom you shall dispossess serve their gods, on the high mountains and the hills and under every green [leafy] tree. You shall tear down their altars and smash their [idolatrous] pillars and burn their Asherim in the fire; you shall cut down the carved and sculpted images of their gods and obliterate their name from that place." Happy and blessed are you, O Israel; who is like you, a people saved by the Lord, the Shield of your help, and the Sword of your majesty! Your enemies will cringe before you, and you will tread on their high places [tramping down their idolatrous altars]."*

2. If we fail to deal with evil alters in our territories this is what will happen according to 1 Kings 3:3 *"And Solomon loved the Lord, walking in the statutes of his father David, except that he sacrificed and burned incense at the high places".*

"Beware that your hearts are not deceived, and that you do not turn away [from the Lord] and serve other gods and worship them, or [else] the Lord's anger will be kindled and burn against you, and He will shut up the heavens so that there

will be no rain and the land will not yield its fruit; and you will perish quickly from the good land which the Lord is giving you.

"Therefore, you shall impress these words of mine on your heart and on your soul, and tie them as a sign on your hand, and they shall be as bands (frontals, frontlets) on your forehead. You shall teach them [diligently] to your children [impressing God's precepts on their minds and penetrating their hearts with His truths], speaking of them when you sit in your house and when you walk along the road and when you lie down and when you rise up." Deuteronomy 11:16-19.

3.   Some churches are built on evil altars to pull crowd, and some secretly pledge allegiance to witches, evil powers or occultic societies for connections and monetary benefits. *"Now this came about because the Israelites had sinned against the Lord heir God, who had brought them up from the land of Egypt, from under the hand of Pharaoh king of Egypt; and they had feared [and worshiped] other gods and walked in the customs of the [pagan] nations whom the Lord had driven out before the sons (descendants) of Israel, and in the pagan customs of the kings of Israel which they had introduced. The Israelites ascribed things to the Lord their God which were not true.*

They built for themselves high places [of worship] in all their towns, from [the lonely] lookout tower to the [populous] fortified city. They set up for themselves sacred pillars (memo-rial stones) and Asherim on every high hill and under every green tree. There they burned incense on all the high places, just as the [pagan] nations whom the Lord had deported before them; and they did evil and contemptible things, provoking the Lord [to anger]. And they served idols, of which the Lord had said to them, "You shall not do this thing." 2 Kings 17:7-12.

4.   All those who service, consult, and worship evil altars

daily provoke the Lord to jealousy as we serve a God who requires and rewards commitment, dedication, and loyalty.

"He also drove out the nations before the sons of Israel and allotted their land as an inheritance, measured out and Partitioned; And He had the tribes of Israel dwell in their tents [the tents of those who had been dispossessed]. Yet they tempted and rebelled against the Most High God and did not keep His testi-monies (laws). They turned back and acted unfaith-fully like their fathers; They were twisted like a warped bow [that will not respond to the archer's aim]. For they provoked Him to [righteous] anger with their high places [devoted to idol worship] and moved Him to jealousy with their carved images [by denying Him the love, worship, and obedience that is rightfully and uniquely His]. When God heard this, He was filled with [righteous] wrath; And utterly rejected Israel, [greatly hating her ways], So that He abandoned the tabernacle at Shiloh, the tent in which He had dwelled among men."
Psalm 78:55-60.

5.   If we fail to act now and repent, God will act to defend His holy name, and every one of us will feel the pain.

"Son of man, set your face against the mountains of Israel and prophesy against them, and say, 'You mountains of Israel, hear the word of the Lord GOD! Thus says the Lord GOD to the mountains and the hills, to the ravines and the valleys: "Behold, I Myself am going to bring a sword on you, and I will destroy your high places [of idolatrous worship], and your altars will become deserted and your pillars for sun-worship will be smashed in pieces; and I will throw down your slain in front of your idols [that cannot bring them back to life]. I will also lay the dead bodies of the children of Israel in front of their [Canaanite] idols; and I will scatter your bones all around your altars. Everywhere you live, the cities will become waste and the high places will become deserted, so that your altars may bear their guilt and become deserted, your idols may be broken

and destroyed, your incense altars [for sun-worship] may be cut down, and your works may be blotted out." Ezekiel 6:2-6.

We are All Connected to Altars

Almost everyone in Africa is connected to evil altars in one way or another, directly or indirectly, through our ancestors, idol worship heritage, and evil foundation. When we read about God's anger and how He said He would bring the sword against those who worship idols [anything that takes the place of God in our lives], we ought to fall on our knees, cry out to God, and weep in repentance. Repentance is the key to breaking free from the power of evil alters. Ge reconnected to the Lord to join the path to freedom from idol worship and be free from wrong connections by moving from fear to faith. We must embrace God's love and trust God above all else.

"When the king heard the words of the Law, he tore his clothes. Then the king commanded Hilkiah, Ahikam the son of Shaphan, Abdon the son of Micah, Shaphan the scribe, and Asaiah a servant of the king, saying, "Go, inquire of the Lord for me and for those who are left in Israel and in Judah in regard to the words of the book which has been found; for great is the wrath of the Lord which has been poured out on us because our fathers have not kept and obeyed the word of the Lord, to act in accordance with everything that is written in this book." So Hilkiah and those whom the king had told went to Huldah the prophetess, the wife of Shallum the son of Tokhath, the son of Hasrah, keeper of the wardrobe (now she lived in Jerusalem, in the Second Quarter); and they spoke to her about this. And she answered them, "Thus says the Lord, the God of Israel: Tell the man who sent you to me, thus says the Lord: Behold, I am bringing evil on this place and on its inhabitants, all the curses that are written in the book which they have read in the presence of the king of Judah. Because they have abandoned (rejected) Me and have burned incense to other gods, in order to provoke Me to anger with all the works of their

hands, My wrath will be poured out on this place, and it will not be extinguished." 2 Chronicles 34: 19-25.

Let's Do What King Josiah Did and Pray Mercy

"Josiah brought out the Asherah from the house of the Lord to the Brook Kidron outside Jerusalem, and burned it there, and ground it to dust, and threw its dust on the graves of the common people [who had sacrificed to it]. And he tore down the houses of the [male] cult prostitutes, which were at the house (temple) of the Lord, where the women were weaving [tent] hangings for the Asherah [shrines].

Then Josiah brought all the [idolatrous] priests from the cities of Judah, and desecrated the high places where the priests had burned incense [to idols], from Geba to Beersheba, [that is, north to south]; and he tore down the high places of the gates which were at the entrance of the gate of Joshua the governor of the city, which were on one's left at the city gate. However, the priests of the high places were not allowed to go up to the altar of the Lord in Jerusalem [to serve], but they ate unleavened bread among their brothers. Josiah also defiled Topheth, which is in the Valley of Ben-hinnom (son of Hinnom), so that no man could make his son or his daughter pass through the fire [as a burnt offering] for Molech.

And he got rid of the horses that the kings of Judah had given [in worship] to the sun at the entrance of the house of the Lord, by the chamber of Nathan-melech the official, which was in the annex; and he burned the chariots of the sun. The altars [dedicated to the starry host of heaven] which were on the roof, the upper chamber of Ahaz, which the kings of Judah had made, and the altars which Manasseh had made in the two courtyards of the house of the Lord, the king tore down; and he smashed them there and threw their dust into the Brook Kidron." 2 Kings 23: 6-13.

Replace Destroyed Evil Altars with New Altars to the Lord

*"Then Elijah said to all the people, "Come near to me."
So, all the people approached him. And he repaired and rebuilt
the [old] altar of the Lord that had been torn down [by
Jezebel]. Then Elijah took twelve stones in accordance with the
number of the tribes of the sons of Jacob, to whom the word of
the Lord had come, saying, "Israel shall be your name." So,
with the stones Elijah built an altar in the name of the Lord.*

*He made a trench around the altar large enough to
hold two measures of seed. Then he laid out the wood and cut
the ox in pieces and laid it on the wood. And he said, "Fill four
pitchers with water and pour it on the burnt offering and the
wood." And he said, "Do it the second time." And they did it
the second time. And he said, "Do it the third time." And they
did it a third time. The water flowed around the altar, and he
also filled the trench with water. At the time of the offering of
the evening sacrifice, Elijah the prophet approached [the altar]
and said, "O Lord, the God of Abraham, Isaac, and Israel
(Jacob), let it be known today that You are God in Israel and
that I am Your servant and that I have done all these things at
Your word. Answer me, O Lord, answer me, so that this people
may know that You, O Lord, are God, and that You have turned
their hearts back [to You]." Then the fire of the Lord fell and
con-sumed the burnt offering and the wood, and even the stones
and the dust; it also licked up the water in the trench. When all
the people saw it, they fell face downward; and they said, "The
Lord, He is God! The Lord, He is God!"* 1 Kings 18:30-39.

Be a Clean Altar Yourself for the Holy Spirit

Our heart is the altar/throne of the Holy Spirit. This is only
true when we completely surrender ourselves and all areas of
our lives to the control of the Holy Spirit according 1
Corinthians 6:19 *"Do you not know that your body is a temple
of the Holy Spirit who is within you, whom you have [received
as a gift] from God, and that you are not your own [property]?"*

Chapter 15

Breakthrough Prayers Part 1

"Now therefore, please forgive my sin only this once [more], and pray and entreat the Lord your God, so that He will remove this [plague of] death from me." Exodus 10:17.

PRAYER POINTS — First Things First. Psalms 66: 18. *"If I regard sin and baseness in my heart [that is, if I know it is there and do nothing about it], the Lord will not hear [me]."*
A. Oh Lord, I come to you humbly. Please, forgive me all my sins. Forgive my family all our sins, in Jesus' name.
B. O Lord, I cry out to you today on behalf of my community and city. Please, have mercy on us, turn away your anger, and let your mercy prevail over judgment, in Jesus' name.

Grace to Pray
Deuteronomy 20:1. *"When you go out to battle against your enemies and see horses and chariots and people more numerous than you, do not be afraid of them; for the Lord your God, who brought you up from the land of Egypt, is with you."*
A. Oh Lord, as I go into spiritual warfare right now. Father be with me. I cover my life and family with the blood of Jesus.
B. Father God, please, give me grace to pray my way to breakthrough, and let my prayers not be in vain, in Jesus' name.
C. By the power in the blood of Jesus, I reject fear, I receive boldness, I overcome all hindrances, in Jesus' name.
D. O Lord, as I begin to pray, let no weapon fashioned against my mind prosper; answer me by fire, in Jesus' name.
E. I bind all anti-prayer demons, waiting to hinder my prayers. Today, I will pray and get results, in Jesus' name.
E. I command all monitoring spirits and satanic watcher to be blinded and their evil mirror destroyed, in Jesus name.

Curses

Deuteronomy 27:15-27. *"Cursed is the man who makes a carved or cast image (idol), a repulsive thing to the Lord, the work of the hands of the artisan, and sets it up in secret. All the people shall answer and say, amen. Cursed is he who dishonors (treats with contempt) his father or his mother. And all the people shall say, amen. Cursed is he who moves his neighbor's boundary mark. And all the people shall say, amen. Cursed is he who misleads a blind person on the road. And all the people shall say, amen. Cursed is he who distorts (perverts) the justice due to a stranger, an orphan, and a widow. And all the people shall say, amen.*

Cursed is he who is intimate with his father's [former] wife, because he has violated what belongs to his father. And all the people shall say, amen. Cursed is he who is intimate with any animal.' And all the people shall say, amen. Cursed is he who is intimate with his [half] sister, whether his father's or his mother's daughter. And all the people shall say, amen. Cursed is he who is intimate with his mother-in-law. And all the people shall say, amen. Cursed is he who strikes his neighbor in secret.' And all the people shall say, amen. Cursed is he who accepts a bribe to strike down an innocent person. And all the people shall say, amen."

A. O Lord, by the power in the blood of Jesus, I break every curse hanging over my life and family, in Jesus' name.

B. Today, by the power in the blood of Jesus, I stand in the gap for my community and city, I break all the curses that have been placed on my community and city, in Jesus' name.

C. I sanctify all curse objects in my home, community, and city, with the blood of Jesus, I dedicate them to God, in Jesus' name.

D. I bind all the territorial forces of darkness assigned to enforce curses in my family, and community, I set myself, my family, and my community free from your bondage, in Jesus' name.

E. O Lord, please forgive me for all the curses I have brought on myself by reason of my sins, mistakes, and carelessness. I break all the curses now, in Jesus' name.

F. I renounce and break all the curses I have placed on my spouse and children, directly or indirectly, in Jesus' name.

G. I renounce and cancel all the curses and negative words or evil decrees my parents have spoken over my life in anger because of my offenses or mistakes, in Jesus' name.

Negative Confession

Matthew 12:37 *"For by your words [reflecting your spiritual condition] you will be justified and acquitted of the guilt of sin; and by your words [rejecting Me] you will be condemned and sentenced."*

A. I renounce and cancel all negative confessions that I have made carelessly or in anger, that the forces of darkness are using as access points or ammunition against me and my family, in Jesus' name.

B. I decree and declare, I am not under any curses, I am blessed. From today, I will be above only, never again will I be beneath. I am the head and not the tail, in Jesus' name.

Covenants

Isaiah 28:15. *"Because you have said, "We have made a covenant with death, And with Sheol (the place of the dead) we have made an agreement, When the overwhelming scourge passes by, it will not reach us, for we have made lies our refuge and we have concealed ourselves in deception."*

A. O Lord, today, I break the covenant I may have made with the territorial spirts in charge of my home, community, and city, in Jesus' name.

B. I break and renounce all the covenants my parents or ancestors made on my behalf with the territorial or familiar spirits, and their representatives in my life and family now, in Jesus' name.

C. Today, I renounce and remove my family and I from all the agreements made between the people of my community and city with Satan directly or indirectly, by the power of the blood of Jesus, in Jesus' name.

D. Today, I terminate the activities and operations of territorial spirits in my community and city because of any covenant that was made, in Jesus' name.

E. All the covenants I made with the gods of this land or my community directly or indirectly with any evil spirit through any means, today, by the power in the blood of Jesus, I break them all, in Jesus' name.

F. I break any covenant I may have entered directly or indirectly with any satanic agents or witches through food, spiritual husband, or wife through sex, familiar spirits through false prophets, and water spirits by any means, in Jesus' name.

Evil Altars

Leviticus 9:24. *"Then fire came out from before the Lord and consumed the burnt offering and the portions of fat on the altar; and when all the people saw it, they shouted and fell face downward [in awe and worship]."*

A. O Lord, I command your fire to come down and consume all the evil altars in my father's house, all the altars in my community and this city now, in Jesus' name.

B. All evil altars sponsored, consulted, and manipulated against my destiny, health, and breakthrough, perish by fire now, in Jesus' name.

C. Any altar where my name or my image, the names or images of my spouse and children have been placed, be consumed by fire now, in Jesus' name.

D. Altars of witches and wizards in my community and city, what are you waiting for, perish by fire, in Jesus' name.

Chapter 16

Breakthrough Prayers Part 2

"When the heavens are shut up and there is no rain because they have sinned against You, and they pray toward this place and praise Your name and turn from their sin when You afflict them, then hear in heaven and forgive the sin of Your servants and of Your people Israel; indeed, teach them the good way in which they should walk (live). And send rain on Your land which You have given to Your people as an inheritance." 1 Kings 8:35-36.

Closed Gates and Doors

1. Matthew 16:19. *"I will give you the keys (authority) of the kingdom of heaven; and whatever you bind [forbid, declare to be improper and unlawful] on earth will have [already] been bound in heaven, and whatever you loose [permit, declare lawful] on earth will have [already] been loosed in heaven."*

I put an end to the activities of territorial spirits, and their agents in my home, community, and city, in Jesus' name.

2. Acts 21:30 *"Then the whole city was provoked, Confused, and the people rushed together. They seized Paul and dragged him out of the temple, and immediately the gates were closed."*

A. I use the keys of the kingdom to close the gates of my home, community, and city to wickedness, bad news, and disfavor, in Jesus' name.

B. All the doors of promotion and progress Satan and his evil agents have closed against me and my family, I command them to be opened now, in Jesus' name.

C. I bind the spirit of bad news, disappointment, division, and disunity, tormenting my life and family, I cast you out of my life now, in Jesus' name.

D. I command all the doors to disappoints, division, and disunity, in my family to be closed now, in Jesus' name.

Chains Broken

1. Acts 16:25-27 *"But about midnight when Paul and Silas were praying and singing hymns of praise to God, and the prisoners were listening to them; suddenly there was a great earthquake, so [powerful] that the very foundations of the prison were shaken and at once all the doors were opened and everyone's chains were unfastened."*
A. Chains of darkness, delay and limitation, holding me back and down to one spot, break now, in Jesus' name.
B. Evil chains of near success syndrome that have held me and my family in captivity, break now, in Jesus' name.

2. Psalm 116:16 *"O Lord, truly I am Your servant; I am Your servant, the son of Your handmaid; You have unfastened my chains."*

Any chain on my legs, hands and neck tying me to my past failures, bad friends, and bad habits, break now, in Jesus' name

3. Psalm 116:16 Ezekiel 7:23 *"O Lord, truly I am Your servant; I am Your servant, the son of Your handmaid; You have unfastened my chains. Prepare the chain [for imprisonment], for the land is full of bloody crimes [murders committed under the pretense of civil justice] and the city is full of violence."*

Any chain prepared for me and my family to capture us, because of carelessness, greed, and negative confession, be consumed by fire now, in Jesus' name.

4. Ecclesiastes 7:26 *"And I discovered that [of all irrational sins none has been so destructive in beguiling one away from God as immoral women for] more bitter than death is the woman whose heart is [composed of] snares and nets, and whose hands are chains. Whoever pleases God will escape from her, but the sinner will be taken captive by her [evil]."*

Any man or woman on assignment from hell to chain my hands, my legs, and my neck, you will not succeed, perish by fire, in Jesus's name.

5. Ezekiel 19:9 *"They put him in a cage with hooks and chains and brought him to the king of Babylon; They brought him in hunting nets So that his voice would be heard no more on the mountains of Israel."*

Chains of darkness used to control and manipulate my life and family to silence our voice and turn our glory to shame, break now, in Jesus' name.

6. Acts 12:7 *"Suddenly, an angel of the Lord appeared [beside him] and a light shone in the cell. The angel struck Peter's side and awakened him, saying, "Get up quickly!" And the chains fell off his hands."*

By the power in the blood of Jesus, shed for my freedom, I break free from the chains of sickness, debt, and shame, in Jesus' name.

Prayer for our Churches

1. 1 Corinthians 1:10 *"But I urge you, believers, by the name of our Lord Jesus Christ, that all of you be in full agreement in what you say, and that there be no divisions or factions among you, but that you be perfectly united in your way of thinking and in your judgment [about matters of the faith]."*

Lord, let your unfailing hands bind us together in the love of Jesus Christ, unity, and establish Your peace in my families, jobs, and communities, in Jesus' name.

2. Matthew 16:18 *"And I say to you that you are Peter, and on this rock, I will build My church; and the gates of Hades (death) will not overpower it [by preventing the resurrection of the Christ]."*

A. I dismantle and destroy every network of darkness, gates of opposition fighting against the spiritual growth and development of our churches, in Jesus' name.

B. Rulers of darkness seducing, suppressing, subverting, and suffocating the spiritual hunger, thirst, and zeal of our church members into worldliness, expire by fire, in Jesus' name.

3. Psalm 35:4-5 *"Let those be ashamed and dishonored*

who seek my life; Let those be turned back [in defeat] and humiliated who plot evil against me. Let them be [blown away] like chaff before the wind [worthless, without substance], with the angel of the Lord driving them on."

O Lord, put all the enemies of our churches into confusion, disgrace, and silence them, in Jesus' name.

4. Psalm 125:3, *"For the scepter of wickedness shall not rest on the land of the righteous, so that the righteous will not reach out their hands to do wrong."*

Do not allow the scepter of the wicked to rest upon our churches, any evil hand or scepter resting upon any of our churches today, be consumed by fire, in Jesus' name.

5. Psalm 7:9 *"Oh, let the wickedness of the wicked come to an end, but establish the just; For the righteous God tests the hearts and minds."*

O Lord, from today, I declare and decree, let all the wickedness of the wicked against our churches, come to an end, in Jesus' name.

6. Isaiah 65:23 *"They shall not labor in vain, nor bring forth children for trouble; For they shall be the descendants of the blessed of the Lord, and their offspring with them."*

Lord, I decree, from today, our evangelism, our prayers and discipleship missions will longer br in vain, in Jesus' name.

7. Psalm 90:17 *"And let the [gracious] favor of the Lord our God be on us; Confirm for us the work of our hands— Yes, confirm the work of our hands."*

Lord, surround me and my family with Your endless favor, establish the works of our hands, and confirm your word, pour upon us the showers of blessings, in Jesus' name.

8. Exodus 33:14 (NLT) *"The Lord replied, "I will personally go with you, Moses, and I will give you rest—everything will be fine for you."*

O Lord, give me rest from disappointments, fear, lack, and stress, in Jesus' name.

9. Isaiah 43:19 *"Listen carefully, I am about to do a new*

thing, now it will spring forth; Will you not be aware of it? I will even put a road in the wilderness, Rivers in the desert."

O Lord, do something new and great in my life, give me a testimony that will silence anyone doubting your power to deliver and your ability to make me great, in Jesus' name.

10. Matthew 19:26 *"But Jesus looked at them and said, "With people [as far as it depends on them] it is impossible, but with God all things are possible."*

Lord, with You, all things are possible, by your mercy, turn all my impossibilities into possibilities, in Jesus' name.

11. Acts 4: 27-31 *"For in this city there were gathered together against Your holy Servant Jesus, whom You anointed, both Herod and Pontius Pilate, along with the Gentiles and the peoples of Israel, to do whatever Your hand and Your purpose predestined [before the creation of the world] to occur [and so without knowing it, they served Your own purpose]. And now, Lord, observe their threats [take them into account] and grant that Your bond-servants may declare Your message [of salvation] with great confidence, while You extend Your hand to heal, and signs and wonders (attesting miracles) take place through the name [and the authority and power] of Your holy Servant and Son Jesus." And when they had prayed, the place where they were meeting together was shaken [a sign of God's presence]; and they were all filled with the Holy Spirit and began to speak the word of God with boldness and courage."*

A. O Lord, arise on behalf of your church, let your counsel and purpose concerning the churches in our communities, begin to manifest like never, in Jesus' name.

B. Lord of heaven and earth, stretch forth Your hands to do great and mighty miracles, signs, and wonders, in our churches more than ever, in Jesus' name.

C. O Lord, grant us the boldness and the courage to preach and exercise the authority of Your holy word over our communities, in Jesus' name.

12. Ephesians 4:11-12 *"And [His gifts to the church were*

varied and] He Himself appointed some as apostles [special messengers, representatives], some as prophets [who speak a new message from God to the people], some as evangelists [who spread the good news of salvation], and some as pastors and teachers [to shepherd and guide and instruct], [and He did this] to fully equip and perfect the saints (God's people) for works of service, to build up the body of Christ [the church]."

O Lord, deliver our church leaders from greed, lust, and pride, that they may fulfil Your call upon their lives without satanic interference, manipulation, and distractions, in Jesus' name.

13. John 17: 20-21 *"I do not pray for these alone [it is not for their sake only that I make this request], but also for [all] those who [will ever] believe and trust in Me through their message, that they all may be one; just as You, Father, are in Me and I in You, that they also may be one in Us, so that the world may believe [without any doubt] that You sent Me."*

14. Habakkuk 3:2 *"O Lord, I have heard the report about You and I fear. O Lord, revive Your work in the midst of the years, In the midst of the years make it known; In wrath [earnestly] remember compassion and love."*

O Lord, revive your work in our hands, revive our individual churches, whatever we have done to offender you, Father, in wrath, remember mercy, in Jesus' name.

Chapter 17

Possessing Your Territory Prayers

"If I shut up the heavens so that no rain falls, or if I command locusts to devour the land, or if I send pestilence and plague among My people, and My people, who are called by My Name, humble themselves, and pray and seek (crave, require as a necessity) My face and turn from their wicked ways, then I will hear [them] from heaven, and forgive their sin and heal their land." 2 Chronicles 7:13-14.

Scriptural Prayer

1. Psalm 107: 8. *"Oh, that men would give thanks to the Lord for His goodness, and for His wonderful works to the children of men."*

Lord, I thank You for Your unfailing love and for all the wonderful things you have done for my family and community, in Jesus' name.

2. Proverbs 28: 13 *"He who covers his sins will not prosper, but whoever confesses and forsakes them will have mercy."*

Father, I confess today that I am a sinner. I have sinned against you knowingly and unknowingly. O Lord, have mercy on me and forgive my sins. Do not let my sins be a hindrance to my breakthrough, in Jesus' Name.

3. 1 John 5: 14. *"Now this is the confidence that we have in Him, that if we ask anything according to His will, He hears us."*

Lord, as I begin to pray, give me grace to pray with confidence and by faith. Please, let my sacrifices of prayer today not be in vain, in Jesus' name.

4. Ephesians 1: 3. *"Blessed be the God and Father of our*

Lord Jesus Christ, who has blessed us with every spiritual blessing in the heavenly places in Christ."

I decree the manifestation of all of God's blessings and favor in my life physically and spiritually, in Jesus' name.

5. Isaiah 54: 17. *"No weapon formed against you shall prosper, and every tongue which rises against you in judgment you shall condemn. This is the heritage of the servants of the Lord, and their righteousness is from Me," says the Lord."*

I come against all the arrows and traps that the agents of darkness have shot and set to destroy or hinder my glory from manifesting, in Jesus' name.

6. Revelations 12: 11. *"And they overcame him by the blood of the Lamb and by the word of their testimony, and they did not love their lives to the death."*

I come against every manipulation of the powers of darkness in every area of my life, family, and community. I overcome them today by the blood of Jesus, in Jesus' name.

7. Ezekiel 34:26. *"I will make them and the places all around My hill a blessing; and I will cause showers to come down in their season; there shall be showers of blessing."*

Almighty God, turn my community and city into the hill of blessing, shower me with blessings that cannot be hidden, or disputed, in Jesus' name.

8. Job 36: 11 *"If they obey and serve Him, they shall spend their days in prosperity, and their years in pleasures."*

O Lord, give me the grace to walk in obedience to your word, so I can spend the rest of my life in peace, good health, and prosperity, in Jesus' name.

9. Isaiah 45: 2 *"I will go before you and make the crooked places straight; I will break in pieces the gates of bronze and cut the bars of iron."*

A. In the name that is above all names, I command the gates of limitation and opposition to my lifting, be destroyed to pieces. Way Maker, go before me, and make all my crooked ways straight for me, in Jesus' name.

B. By the authority vested in me as a child of God, I command the chains of limitation, delay, and setback in any area of my life be removed now, in Jesus' name.

10. Isaiah 45: 3. *"I will give you the treasures of darkness and hidden riches of secret places, that you may know that I, the Lord, who call you by your name, Am the God of Israel."*

A. Today, I decree, all the blessings and opportunities the powers of darkness have stolen from me and my family, be restored now, in Jesus's name.

B. I command my spiritual eyes to be opened, my physical eyes to be empowered, and my eyes of understanding to be enlightened to recognize hidden treasures, opportunities, and riches, in Jesus' name.

11. Proverbs 4: 7-8. *"Wisdom is the principal thing; Therefore, get wisdom. and in all your getting, get understanding. Exalt her, and she will promote you; She will bring you honor, when you embrace her."*

A. O Lord, give me the wisdom I need to create wealth, to invest wisely, and breakthrough in my career, ministry, education, and marriage, in Jesus' name.

B. O Lord, please endow me with divine understanding and empower me with great grace for greater workers to fulfil the great commission with signs and wonders following, in Jesus' name.

C. Today, I receive the wisdom to make money my servant, and the understanding to manage money and my family for your glory, in Jesus' name.

12. Deuteronomy 28: 12 *"The Lord will open to you His good treasure, the heavens, to give the rain to your land in its season, and to bless all the work of your hand. You shall lend to many nations, but you shall not borrow."*

A. O Lord, open the way for my helpers of destiny to locate me, I set my helpers of destiny free from limitations, and setback, and procrastination, in Jesus' name.

B. O Lord, let the heavens above me be opened to give me the showers of blessings without ceasing, in Jesus' name.

C. From today, I refuse to eat the bread of sorrow and drink the waters of affliction, deliver me from the stronghold of debt and lack, in Jesus' name.

D. O Lord, bless the works of my hands, from today let the works of my hands, and investments begin to experience divine favor, multiplication, and fruitfulness, in Jesus' name.

13. Isaiah 43: 19 *"Behold, I will do a new thing, now it shall spring forth; Shall you not know it? I will even make a road in the wilderness and rivers in the desert."*

A. Almighty God, by your strong and mighty hands, move me upward and forward to greater heights, to new possibilities and into the realm of greatness, in Jesus' name.

B. O Lord, where there seems to be no way, make a way for me, create a way for me out of the wilderness, and rivers in my areas of dryness physically and spiritually, in Jesus' name.

14. Proverbs 16: 32 *"He who is slow to anger is better than the mighty, and he who rules his spirit than he who takes a city."*

O Lord, give me the grace to control my emotions, overcome greed, and resist anger, so that none of them will become stumbling blocks to my promotion, breakthrough, and favor, in Jesus' name.

15. Philippians 4:13 Psalm 59:1-2. *"I can do all things through Christ who strengthens me. Deliver me from mine enemies, O my God: defend me from them that rise up against me. Deliver me from the workers of iniquity and save me from bloody men."*

A. My Father, deliver me from all my enemies, unfriendly friends, and from the traps, manipulations, and deception of false prophets and pastors, in Jesus' name.

B. O Lord, deliver me and my family from the hands of human traders, who traffic their fellow men for money, and rituals, in Jesus' name.

17. Psalm 35:1 *"Plead my cause, O Lord, with those who strive with me; Fight against those who fight against me."*

Rock of Ages, arise and fight against all those who are fighting against my health, peace, and progress, in Jesus' name.

18. Daniel 6:3 *"Then this Daniel distinguished himself above the governors and satraps, because an excellent spirit was in him; and the king gave thought to setting him over the whole realm."*

O Lord, from today, let your favor distinguish me from all the ungodly around me, let your spirit of excellence take over my life and everything that concerns me, in Jesus' name.

19. Psalm 25:1-2 *"Unto thee, O Lord, do I lift up my soul. O my God, I trust in thee: let me not be ashamed, let not mine enemies triumph over me."*

O Lord, you are the defender of the weak, let me not be put to shame, and let not mine enemies' triumph over me ever again, in Jesus' name.

20. Jeremiah 30:17 *"For I will restore health unto thee, and I will heal thee of thy wounds, saith the Lord."*

Balm of Gilead, heal all my mental, physical, and spiritual wounds, renew my strength, and make me completely whole, in Jesus' name.

21. Job 5:12 *"He frustrates the devices of the crafty, So that their hands cannot carry out their plans."*

O Lord, frustrate all the devices and schemes of the wicked against me, let the hands lifted against me become weak and wither, in Jesus' name.

22. Proverbs 16:3. *"Commit your works to the Lord, and your thoughts will be established."*

O Lord, I commit my children, and my plans for them into your hands, grant me favor and establish my plans with success, bless my children and make them great, in Jesus' name.

Erase Your Family Name from Evil Altars

A. By the power in the blood of Jesus, today, I erase my name, the names of my children, and that of spouse from all satanic altars or shrines, in the air, land, and sea, in Jesus' name.

B. All the evil altars in the air, land, and sea, speaking evil and calamities into my life and family, be silenced forever, in Jesus' name.

C. O Lord, I decree and declare, all the accusations and evil reports brought against me and my family on any altar in my community and city, let your fire fall from heaven and settle the matter now, in Jesus' name.

D. Every demonic embargo placed over my life, placed over my family, and community by the powers of darkness, what are you waiting for, be removed by fire, in Jesus' name.

F. Yokes of darkness used by the enemies of progress to suppress, oppress, and depress my life, be broken, in Jesus' name.

G. Powers or the air, powers of the land, and powers of the water, today, I destroy your stronghold over my life, over my family and over my community, in Jesus' name.

Chapter 18

Prayer for Our Territories

"Jabez was more honorable than his brothers; but his mother named him Jabez, saying, "Because I gave birth to him in pain." Jabez cried out to the God of Israel, saying, "Oh that You would indeed bless me and enlarge my border [property], and that Your hand would be with me, and You would keep me from evil so that it does not hurt me!" And God granted his request." 1 Chronicles 4:9-10.

Scriptural Prayer Points for Our Territories

1. Isaiah 14:5 *"The Lord has broken the staff of the wicked, the scepter of the [tyrant] rulers."*

O Lord, I declare, and I decree, I command the staff, scepter, and evil yoke of the wicked over my family, city, and nation to break to pieces, in Jesus' name.

2. Mark 4:39 NKJV *"Then He arose and rebuked the wind, and said to the sea, "Peace, be still!" And the wind ceased and there was a great calm."*

The wind of darkness, opposition, and disaster, blowing away the blessings and breakthroughs of my family, city, and nation, cease now, in Jesus' name.

3. 1 Chronicles 29:12 *"Both riches and honor come from You, and You rule over all. In Your hand is power and might; and it is in Your hands to make great and to give strength to everyone."*

O Lord, I know You can do all things, by Your mercy, make me great, rich, and honor me, in Jesus' name.

4. Psalm 105:40 *"The Israelites asked, and He brought quail, and satisfied them with the bread of heaven."*

God Almighty, by your mercy, supply my family, city, and nation with all the resources we need to be great, rich, and powerful, in Jesus' name.

5. Psalm 105:24 *"There the Lord greatly increased [the number of] His people and made them more powerful than their enemies."*

O Lord, increase, and prosper your churches in our community, cities, and nations, make us stronger than our enemies, in Jesus' name.

6. Psalm 105:44 *"He gave them the lands of the nations [of Canaan], so that they would possess the fruits of those peoples' labor. "*

I command the goodness, and profits from our natural resources on our land be restored back to us, in Jesus' name.

7. Psalm 105:32 *"He gave them hail for rain, with flaming fire in their land."*

O Lord, all the people in high places working against and troubling the peace and prosperity of my nation, give them hail for rain and flaming fire for their wickedness and corruption, in Jesus' name.

8. Zechariah 1: 21 *"I asked, "What are these [horns and crafts-men] coming to do?" And he said, "These are the horns (powers) that have scattered Judah so that no man raised up his head [because of the suffering inflicted by the Gentile nations]. But these craftsmen have come to terrify them and make them panic, and throw down the horns of the nations who have lifted up their horns against the land of Judah in order to scatter it."*

Today, in the name that is above all names, I bind the principalities, powers, rulers of darkness, and spiritual wickedness on assignment to destroy the joy and peace of my family, my city, and nation, be consumed by fire, in Jesus' name.

9. Daniel 7:3, 11 *"And four great beasts, each different from the other, were coming up out of the sea [in succession]. Then I kept looking because of the sound of the great and boastful words which the horn was speaking. I kept looking until the beast was slain, and its body destroyed and given to be burned with fire."*

In the name that is above all names, I bind the beast of the land, beast of the sea, beast of the air, and assigned territorial beast troubling and plaguing my family, community, and nation, be destroyed by fire, in Jesus' name.

10. Psalm 18:14 *"He sent out His arrows and scattered them; and He sent an abundance of lightning flashes and confused and routed them [in defeat]."*

O Lord, I release the arrows of fire into the camps of the agents of darkness in my nation, and I command their evil network to scatter by fire, in Jesus' name.

11. Job 18:5 *"Indeed, the light of the wicked will be put out, and the flame of his fire will not shine.*

O Lord, I decree in the name above all names, let the evil and the cloud of the wicked over my community be removed now, and let their glory turned to shame, in Jesus' name.

12. Psalm 34:19 *"Many hardships and perplexing circums-tances confront the righteous, but the Lord rescues him from them all."*

O Lord, by your mercy, deliver my family, city, and nation from economic hardship, inflation, and evil occurrences, in Jesus' name.

13. Isaiah 9:2 *"The people who walk in [spiritual] darkness will see a great Light; those who live in the dark land, the Light will shine on them."*

O Lord: Shine your light upon my family, city, and nation, I command, the stronghold of darkness over my family, my city, and my nation, be broken now, in Jesus' name.

14. 2 Chronicles 7:14 *"And My people, who are called by My Name, humble themselves, and pray and seek (crave, require as a necessity) My face and turn from their wicked ways, then I will hear [them] from heaven, and forgive their sin and heal their land."*

O Lord, please forgive the sins of our leaders, neighbors, and heal our land, in Jesus' name.

15. Isaiah 54:17 *"No weapon that is formed against you will*

succeed; And every tongue that rises against you in judgment you will condemn. This [peace, righteousness, security, and triumph over opposition] is the heritage of the servants of the Lord, and this is their vindication from Me," says the Lord."

All the weapons of darkness formed against my family, city, and nation, I decree, you will not succeed, in Jesus' name.

16. Psalm 32:7 *"You are my hiding place; You, Lord, protect me from trouble; You surround me with songs and shouts of deliverance. Selah."*

O Lord, by your mercy, protect my family, city and nation from reproach and shame, surround us with the songs of deliverance, in Jesus' name.

17. Psalm 85:6 *"Will You not revive us and bring us to life again, That Your people may rejoice in You?"*

O Lord, send down revival, revive us again, so our families, cities, and nations will rejoice in You, in Jesus' name.

18. Revelation 21:4. *"And God shall wipe away all tears from their eyes; and there shall be no more death, neither sorrow, nor crying, neither shall there be any more pain: for the former things are passed away.'*

O Lord, have compassion on me and my family, wipe away our tears and shame, let evil and bad news be far away from me and my family, in Jesus' name.

19. Romans 8:28 *"And we know that all things work together for good to those who love God, to those who are the called according to His purpose."*

I declare and decree, everything in heaven, on earth and under the earth that has been working against me, from today begin to work together for my good, favor, breakthrough, promotion, and blessing, in Jesus' name.

20. Job 24:13 *"Others have been with those who rebel against the light; They do not want to know its ways nor stay in its paths.*

O Lord, by your mercy, restore back to the fold all backsliders, deliver them from the grip of worldliness, and from the power darkness, in Jesus' name.

21. Jeremiah 3:22 *"Return, O faithless sons," [says the Lord], I will heal your unfaithfulness. [They answer] Behold, we come to You, for You are the Lord our God."*

O Lord, we have all been unfaithful to You one way or the other, today Lord individually and collectively we repent, please, heal our unfaithfulness and restore us back to our first love, in Jesus' name.

22. Joel 2:25 *"And I will compensate you for the years that the swarming locust has eaten, the creeping locust, the stripping locust, and the gnawing locust—My great army which I sent among you."*

O Lord, have compassion on my family and our community, please restore and compensate us for all the years we have lost to disappointments, delays, and limitations, in Jesus' name.

About the Author

Joseph Blessing Omosigho — has been shepherding God's flocks for more than twenty-five years. Joseph has traveled far and wide training servant leaders in Christian leadership. Joseph is an experienced preacher, and an extra-ordinary teacher of the uncompromising word of God, serving to reach the world with the surpassing love of Jesus Christ. Apostle Joseph is married to pastor Gloria, blessed with four children: David, Samuel, Hannah, and Moses. The Lord met Joseph in 1988, wandering aimlessly in sin, worldliness, and paganism, and brought him to the cross through the power of the Holy Spirit, where he encountered God's love and became a born-again Christian.

Once Joseph repented, he gave up paganism and stopped worshiping man-made gods to worship the true and only one unfailing living God. God saved Joseph from a very devoted pagan family. Joseph was rejected and disowned by his father after giving his life to Jesus Christ. God became his father from that day forward. God has used Brother Joseph to write many life-changing inspirational and Spirit-filled books, gospel songs, and movie scripts. You can invite Apostle Joseph to minister God's living word at your ministry, church, outreach, or gospel meetings only as the Lord leads. Joseph is a full gospel preacher and teacher of God's word. If your people need to hear the truth of God's word void of fleshly manipulation, con games, and deception, call, or write Apostle Joseph today.

Tel: 214-994-8080 or Email: ministryofchrist@gmail.com
You can order Pastor Joseph's books from amazon.com.